TEACHER RECRUITMENT, RETENTION AND CAREER PROGRESSION

Edited by **THE CHARTERED COLLEGE OF TEACHING**

TEACHER RECRUITMENT, RETENTION AND CAREER PROGRESSION

A GUIDE FOR SCHOOL LEADERS

1 Oliver's Yard
55 City Road
London EC1Y 1SP

2455 Teller Road
Thousand Oaks
California 91320

Unit No 323-333, Third Floor, F-Block
International Trade Tower
Nehru Place, New Delhi – 110 019

8 Marina View Suite 43-053
Asia Square Tower 1
Singapore 018960

Editor: Amy Thornton
Senior project editor: Chris Marke
Cover design: Wendy Scott
Typeset by: C&M Digitals (P) Ltd, Chennai, India

Editorial arrangement © 2026 Chartered College of Teaching.

Introduction Dr Cat Scutt; Chapter 1 Nansi Ellis and Gareth Conyard; Chapter 2 Dr Victoria Cook and Dr Lisa-Maria Müller; Chapter 3 Polly Butterfield-Tracey; Chapter 4 Beng Huat See, Stephen Gorard and Fujia Yang; Chapter 5 Angela Browne and Sufian Sadiq; Chapter 6 Claire O'Neill; Chapter 7 Professor Catherine Lee; Chapter 8 Professor Tanya Ovenden-Hope; Chapter 9 Lucy Rose and Lindsay Patience; Chapter 10 Yamina Bibi.

Apart from any fair dealing for the purposes of research or private study, or criticism or review, as permitted under the Copyright, Designs and Patents Act 1988, this publication may be reproduced, stored or transmitted in any form, or by any means, only with the prior permission in writing of the publishers, or in the case of reprographic reproduction, in accordance with the terms of licences issued by the Copyright Licensing Agency. Enquiries concerning reproduction outside those terms should be sent to the publishers.

Library of Congress Control Number: 2025939954

British Library Cataloguing in Publication data

A catalogue record for this book is available from the British Library

ISBN 978-1-0362-1238-4
ISBN 978-1-0362-1237-7 (pbk)

CONTENTS

About the authors   vii

Introduction – teacher recruitment, retention and
career progression: why it matters   1
Dr Cat Scutt

Part 1   Understanding the challenges of teacher recruitment and retention   7

1. Education policy and professional development: understanding key legislative shifts and policy initiatives   9
Nansi Ellis and Gareth Conyard

2. Teacher professionalism: the importance of professional identity and autonomy for retention and career progression   23
Dr Victoria Cook and Dr Lisa-Maria Müller

3. The challenges schools face in recruiting teachers: organisational cultures and the complexity of the ITT market   35
Polly Butterfield-Tracey

4. Understanding the under-representation of minority ethnic teachers   49
Beng Huat See, Stephen Gorard and Fujia Yang

Part 2   Inclusive leadership: strategies for supporting diverse staff teams   67

5. Inclusive leadership: addressing systemic barriers to support teachers from minority ethnic backgrounds   69
Angela Browne and Sufian Sadiq

6   Recruiting and supporting neurodivergent teachers
    by developing an inclusive work environment   78
    Claire O'Neill

7   Recruiting and retaining LGBTQ+ teachers through inclusive leadership 91
    Professor Catherine Lee

**Part 3   Building supportive work environments: fostering career
           progression for all   103**

8   Supporting teacher retention and career progression:
    fostering early career teacher self-efficacy through reflective
    practice and professional development   105
    Professor Tanya Ovenden-Hope

9   Flexible working practices to support recruitment, retention
    and career development   122
    Lucy Rose and Lindsay Patience

10 Addressing workload and supporting teacher wellbeing   134
    Yamina Bibi

Index   146

ABOUT THE AUTHORS

Angela Browne is the founder and CEO of Being Luminary, a global consultancy specialising in diversity, equity and inclusion (DEI) within educational settings. With over two decades of experience in education, including roles as headteacher and interim deputy CEO of a multi-academy trust, she now provides leadership coaching and DEI consulting to organisations worldwide.

Beng Huat See is Professor of Education Research at the School of Education, University of Birmingham, and a fellow of the Academy of Social Sciences and the Royal Society of Arts. Her current research focuses on understanding the complexity of teacher supply internationally and improving diversity in the teaching workforce.

Professor Catherine Lee MBE is Pro Vice-Chancellor and Dean of the Faculty of Arts, Humanities, Education and Social Sciences at Anglia Ruskin University. She is a researcher and adviser on LGBTQ+ inclusion in education. In 2023 Catherine received an MBE for services to equality in education for her leadership development work in schools and universities.

Dr Cat Scutt MBE, Deputy CEO of Education and Research at the Chartered College of Teaching, leads initiatives on teacher development and research engagement. A former English teacher, she received an MBE for services to education in 2021.

Claire O'Neill is an experienced primary teacher, post-primary teacher and teacher-educator based in Ireland. She writes regularly about leadership, inclusive education and neurodiversity-affirmative approaches. Claire is research-active and contributes to several national and international research advisory panels. Claire is multiply neurodivergent and her lived experience informs her professional and academic work.

Fujia Yang is a postgraduate researcher at the School of Education, University of Birmingham. Her research explores the use of educational technology in improving students' reading behaviours and outcomes.

Gareth Conyard is CEO of the Teacher Development Trust (TDT), a charity dedicated to supporting effective professional development for teachers and leaders. Prior to joining TDT, Gareth had a 19-year career in the civil service, mainly at the Department for Education (DfE).

Lindsay Patience is co-founder of Flexible Teacher Talent, a social enterprise evolving from a Teach First Innovation Series project aiming to improve flexible working opportunities in the education sector in order to retain talented teachers and leaders in our schools. She has worked in London secondary schools since 2006 and first joined the senior leadership team in 2011. After having her first child in 2016 she was shocked by the lack of flexible opportunities available when she wanted to return to work and since then has been working to address this issue. She currently teaches A-level economics part time.

Dr Lisa-Maria Müller, Head of Research at the Chartered College of Teaching, leads research projects, including evaluations of teacher continuing professional development (CPD) and wellbeing. She earned her PhD from the University of Vienna and has taught modern foreign languages in Austria and England.

Lucy Rose is co-founder of Flexible Teacher Talent, a social enterprise born of a desire to see better in a sector which was haemorrhaging talented teachers and leaders at often the most vulnerable times in their lives. Navigating the workplace 'lottery' and working flexibly as an English teacher, she has co-authored *Flex Education: A Practical Guide to Flexible Working in Schools* (2022) and supports teachers and leaders to implement flexible solutions which align with the vision and values of their particular context. She is committed to implementing flexibility which benefits all: staff, the organisation and, most importantly, the students.

Nansi Ellis is an education policy consultant supporting organisations to develop policy, influence and strategy. She is a primary school governor, Trustee of the Association for Citizenship Teaching and Culham St Gabriels and co-author, with Gareth Conyard, of *Improving Education Policy Together* (2024). She was previously Assistant General Secretary at NEU and ATL.

Polly Butterfield-Tracey FCCT is Head of KMT, a leading provider of initial teacher training (ITT) in the South East, and Deputy Director of the Leigh Institute. Previously, she served as Project Director for CESET, a DfE innovation pilot featured in the 2019 Recruitment and Retention Strategy. With a focus on partnerships, she has extensive experience in teacher training and development, collaborating with national and regional organisations. Committed to regional impact, Polly works with numerous schools across Kent and London, driving impactful change through research-informed practice and professional development.

ABOUT THE AUTHORS

Stephen Gorard is Professor of Education and Public Policy at Durham University, Director of the Durham University Evidence Centre for Education, Durham University, a world-renowned social scientist and author of over 1,000 publications. His work is regularly discussed in Parliament and is cited on the websites of thousands of schools in England.

Sufian Sadiq is the Director of Talent and Teaching School at Chiltern Learning Trust, with responsibility for overseeing four school-centred ITT (SCITT) provisions, two regional hub areas in the South East of England, as well as behaviour and attendance hubs. Chiltern Teaching School is one of the largest providers of CPD to the sector nationally. He is a passionate activist within the educational landscape around race, equity and inclusion. He is a serving Ofsted inspector. Sufian is a proud Fellow and President-Elect of the Chartered College of Teaching, as well as a Fellow for the Chartered Institute of Educational Assessors. He plays an active role in numerous charitable organisations as a trustee and also holds key governance roles within educational organisations.

Professor (Dr) Tanya Ovenden-Hope is Dean of Place and Social Purpose and Professor of Education at Plymouth Marjon University. Tanya holds the highest professional status for teaching and learning in all three education sectors (FCCT, FSET and PFHEA). Her research on place-based inequity for schools, teacher recruitment and retention, and teacher professional development has influenced thinking on the way schools access resources. She holds elected and invited roles on the British Educational Research Association (elected council member), International Council in Education for Teaching (Vice-President, Europe) and for the Paul Hamlyn Foundation Teacher Development Fund (Advisory Board Member).

Dr Victoria Cook is Lead Researcher at the Chartered College of Teaching. In collaboration with colleagues at IOE, UCL's Faculty of Education and Society, Victoria is currently managing the scoping phase of an EEF-funded project on the impact of offsite planning, preparation and assessment (PPA) on teacher retention. Prior to joining the college, Victoria worked as a Research Associate at the Faculty of Education, University of Cambridge, for five years on two international dialogue-based research projects. She is a trained geography teacher, and her research interests include cultural literacy and technology-mediated dialogue.

Yamina Bibi FCCT is a former deputy headteacher, English teacher, consultant and currently an education project specialist for the Chartered College of Teaching and Chiltern Learning Trust. Yamina is also author of *The Little Guide for Teachers: Thriving in Your First Years of Teaching* (2024). Additionally, Yamina is co-founder of South Asian Educators' Network, an associate, trainer and coach for Diverse Educators and a #WomenEd network leader.

INTRODUCTION

TEACHER RECRUITMENT, RETENTION AND CAREER PROGRESSION: WHY IT MATTERS

DR CAT SCUTT

It will come as no surprise to anyone reading this book that the education system in England currently faces significant challenges in maintaining an adequate supply of teachers, and has done so for a number of years. Teacher workforce data indicates that teacher supply is in a critical state, with ITT recruitment falling below target in many subjects over successive years. The situation is exacerbated by persistent teacher retention challenges, with more and more teachers leaving the profession – including early in their careers. The latest ITT application data and research around teacher job satisfaction, meanwhile, suggest that significant improvements in the near future are unlikely, so even those of you picking up this book in future years are likely seeing these challenges around teacher supply continuing. With leadership unions also reporting fewer teachers having a desire to progress into senior leadership roles, the picture around school workforce looks bleak.

These challenges in teacher supply represent a substantial risk to the quality of education. We know the importance of high-quality teachers for pupil outcomes, particularly for children and young people from disadvantaged backgrounds. Teacher supply issues, meanwhile, are often particularly acute in schools serving the most disadvantaged communities. As well as a lack of teachers overall, the current teacher recruitment issues affect some subjects more than others, meaning that children are increasingly likely to be taught by non-specialists for some subjects. Challenges around recruitment and retention have a knock-on effect for those teachers that remain, who may be placed under increasing pressure.

While the picture painted here will be very familiar for many of those working in schools in England, the wider UK and beyond, this book seeks to unpack the current situation in further depth, whilst proposing some ways in which these challenges might be addressed.

Across all the chapters in this book, a number of key themes emerge, both around the causes of the recruitment and retention crisis, and the ways in which it may be addressed. While not all of these are directly within the remit of school leadership, many of them are – and they can all be influenced through school leaders' policy advocacy, so raising awareness is key.

POLICY, PRACTICE AND TEACHER PROFESSIONALISM

A first key theme is the impact of policy initiatives and notions of teacher professionalism and identity on teacher recruitment and retention. While the situation in England is not unique, there is no doubt that policy decisions play a key role in influencing teacher recruitment and retention, and policy activity is one of the key levers to improving the current situation. Successive governments have sought to address the growing teacher recruitment and retention challenges through a range of initiatives, including those relating to CPD, training bursaries, workload and more. The early chapters of this book explore some of the history and implications of government policy around the teaching profession, to set the context within which teachers and school leaders are working.

In Chapter 1, Nansi Ellis and Gareth Conyard discuss the historical development of teaching as a profession and the impact of legislative shifts and policy-making on teacher professionalism, a theme that continues into Chapter 2, where Victoria Cook and Lisa-Maria Müller argue that a focus on developing and sustaining teacher professionalism is a central aspect of addressing current recruitment and retention challenges. They introduce the Chartered College of Teaching's model of teacher professionalism, which emphasises cognitive, legal/social and ethical domains, with authority, prestige, esteem and status viewed as outcomes of addressing these features. Finally, teacher professional identity and teacher autonomy are highlighted as crucial for teacher professionalism and retention.

The policy theme continues in the third chapter, as Polly Butterfield-Tracy considers in detail some of the difficulties in teacher recruitment, reflecting on the significant reconfiguration that the ITT market has undergone following a rigorous re-accreditation process, leading to challenges for school leaders in meeting the demands of different ITT providers. Trainee teachers also report difficulties navigating the application process and often experience low morale and high workload. School culture, including workload expectations and teacher wellbeing, significantly impacts the attractiveness of teaching as a profession and a school as an employer. The chapter proposes a solution to this that involves a collaborative approach across schools, universities, ITT providers and teaching school hubs to address these challenges, as well as recommending ways in which school leaders can build local strategic partnerships, create an attractive employer culture, optimise ITT engagement and cultivate a collaborative approach.

We return to policy initiatives, teacher autonomy and identity again in Chapter 8, where Tanya Ovenden-Hope addresses the key issue of attrition of early career teachers (ECTs) and the role and limitations of the Early Career Framework (ECF). The chapter explores the ways in which teacher self-efficacy and job satisfaction are crucial for retention, and how issues such as workload, lack of autonomy and insufficient support can all contribute to teachers leaving the profession. Although the value of the ECF in providing structured support for ECTs is recognised, so too is the need for school leaders to adapt and enhance it to meet the specific needs of their ECTs and school context. The transition to full-time teaching can be a period of *reality shock* characterised by workload intensity, classroom management difficulties and challenges in adapting to school culture. School leaders play a vital role in creating a supportive and inclusive school culture, providing consistent feedback and recognising the contributions of ECTs, and the author proposes a range of practical strategies for school leaders including implementing effective mentoring programmes, designing structured reflective practice opportunities, developing a growth-oriented school culture that fosters self-efficacy and provides time for professional development, and extending support beyond the formal ECF requirements to support long-term retention.

INCLUSIVE SCHOOLS AND INCLUSIVE LEADERSHIP

A second key theme is the need for schools, and the wider education system, to support a diverse workforce by adopting inclusive practices. There is a moral imperative for this work; our teaching workforce should be as inclusive as we seek for our classrooms to be. And, as in the classroom, it is clear that adopting inclusive practices benefits all teachers, not just those who may currently face particular barriers to joining and progressing in the teaching profession. Several chapters focus on some of the groups of teachers who too often face barriers in their careers, and consider some of the changes needed at a system and school level to address these. While the coverage of this book is not exhaustive, and there are many more groups of teachers who face particular challenges that urgently need to be addressed if we wish for teaching to be a truly inclusive profession, these chapters provide an important starting point for thinking about how schools can be more inclusive for all staff members.

In Chapter 4, Beng Huat See, Stephen Gorard and Fujia Yang examine the underrepresentation of minority ethnic teachers in England's teaching workforce, exploring research indicating that applicants from minority ethnic backgrounds face more barriers to success at every stage, from application to training to employment, and highlight the bias embedded within application and assessment processes. They note that while improved working conditions are necessary to benefit all teachers, teachers from minority ethnic backgrounds face the additional burden of dealing with racial discrimination and inequalities, and suggest actions such as addressing implicit bias, closing disparities in entry requirements and increasing the number of minority ethnic school leaders to improve diversity. Supportive school leaders and reducing ethnic segregation in schools are also identified as important for retaining minority ethnic teachers.

Chapter 5 continues this theme, with Angela Browne and Sufian Sadiq discussing how the significant racial inequality in the UK teaching workforce continues across all career stages, particularly in leadership. The chapter explores systemic barriers, including the phenomenon of intellectual racism, whereby minority ethnic teachers may be steered towards pastoral roles rather than teaching and learning leadership. The importance of moving beyond the limiting 'role model' framing of minority ethnic teachers is also discussed, as well as the need to adopt a human-centred approach to leadership, prioritise genuine relationships and actively listen to concerns in order to foster a more inclusive school culture.

In Chapter 6, another aspect of inclusion and its importance in the context of teacher recruitment, retention and career progression is considered, as Claire O'Neill focuses on how school leaders can recruit, support and retain neurodivergent teachers. The chapter introduces the LEARNING Framework as a model to guide school leaders in developing a neurodiversity-informed perspective on inclusion; the author suggests that inclusive advertising, transparent recruitment processes and a willingness to make equitable adjustments are crucial for attracting neurodivergent candidates. Supporting neurodivergent teachers involves developing an inclusive school culture and critically examining language used within the school, as well as honouring neurodivergent expertise and ensuring agency and autonomy in teaching roles – linking back to the first key theme of the book.

Chapter 7 addresses the barriers faced by LGBTQ+ teachers in recruitment, retention and professional progression. Catherine Lee highlights that, despite legal advancements, many LGBTQ+ educators still experience discrimination and cultural challenges, and the legacy of Section 28 continues to impact the confidence of teachers in discussing LGBTQ+ issues; barriers to recruitment include discrimination and a lack of visible LGBTQ+ role models. The author explains how schools can signal inclusivity through visible symbols, inclusive policies and participation in LGBTQ+ awareness events, as well as integrating LGBTQ+ identities and experiences across the curriculum. She shares practical strategies and real-life examples, noting that while teachers should not be coerced into coming out, schools must create safe and supportive environments where they feel comfortable doing so. Finally, she addresses the challenges of navigating potentially conservative stances from school communities and school governors, highlighting the experiences of educators like Andrew Moffat as examples of the challenges school leaders may face in implementing LGBTQ+-inclusive policies and the importance of supportive leadership.

A final aspect of inclusive practice, which also links back to the theme of policy, comes later in the book in Chapter 9, where Lindsay Patience and Lucy Rose explore the potential of flexible working as a tool to attract and retain educators. Despite perceived barriers, thoughtful and proactive implementation of flexible working can positively impact pupil outcomes and support retention not just for parents or those with caring responsibilities, but also for those early in their career, suggesting that flexibility at the start of teachers' careers might help mitigate overwhelm and promote retention. As an area currently being explored widely in policy and research, the authors argue that flexible working is a high priority now and explore the changing landscape of flexible working, as well as how it might look in different school settings. They encourage school leaders to commit to flexibility, involve staff in conversations about their needs, and trial and monitor different approaches.

WORKLOAD, WELLBEING, PROFESSIONAL DEVELOPMENT AND COACHING

Another set of themes relate to some of the other drivers of poor teacher retention and possible means of addressing these. We know that the reasons teachers leave the profession are many and varied, but commonly identified drivers of teacher attrition include unmanageable workload, poor wellbeing and pupil behaviour. These are complex issues: for example, teacher workload is not just about the number of hours teachers work, but also the nature of the tasks that they are asked to do and the extent to which these feel valuable for pupils and intellectually and professionally satisfying for teachers. These specific drivers of teacher attrition and the steps that schools may take to address them, including changes to school policies and practice, are discussed in depth by Yamina Bibi in Chapter 10.

Finally, the value of CPD, teacher collaboration and coaching and mentoring are clear themes across the whole book. Common reasons that teachers report choosing teaching as a career include a desire to make a difference, a desire to work with children and young people, a passion for their subject and, crucially, the belief that they will be good at it. Through effective CPD and opportunities to develop with colleagues, teachers can be empowered to become highly effective practitioners and to have confidence in their own practice, building their job satisfaction and keeping them in the profession – enabling them to continue to develop their craft as expert teachers over time.

This is clear in the practical approaches that Yamina Bibi suggests in the final chapter to address teacher retention challenges, which include opportunities for professional development, coaching and mentoring for teachers to develop powerful collaboration. Victoria Cook and Lisa-Maria Müller make similar arguments in Chapter 2 around teacher professionalism as they highlight the pivotal role that professional development plays in raising the status of the profession and the impact it may have on recruitment and retention rates. They also share examples of how personalised approaches to CPD can support mid-career teachers who wish to develop their classroom expertise rather than progressing into traditional leadership roles, as well as exploring how collaborative approaches to CPD, such as journal clubs, can foster both individual and collective expertise, efficacy and autonomy.

Overall, then, this book aims to equip school leaders with a deeper understanding of the challenges in teacher recruitment and retention and the potential causes of different issues, alongside practical strategies for fostering inclusive environments and supporting the professional growth and wellbeing of all teachers. Schools alone cannot solve the recruitment and retention crisis. There is a clear role here for policy-makers and there are also wider issues that are affecting teacher recruitment and retention that are not addressed in depth here, including teacher pay and the impact of the accountability system. But the research is also clear on the power of school culture and the role that leaders play in this. By addressing issues around professionalism, identity, autonomy, workload, diversity and flexible working as far as is possible in their own settings, school leaders can start to work towards creating a more sustainable and rewarding profession for teachers, no matter the stage of their careers.

PART 1
UNDERSTANDING THE CHALLENGES OF TEACHER RECRUITMENT AND RETENTION

1

EDUCATION POLICY AND PROFESSIONAL DEVELOPMENT

UNDERSTANDING KEY LEGISLATIVE SHIFTS AND POLICY INITIATIVES

NANSI ELLIS AND GARETH CONYARD

INTRODUCTION

The professional development of teachers – from initial training through to career development and advanced study – has gradually but increasingly come under the purview of government over the last 80 years. This means tighter government control at the same time as the general quality of teachers (and teacher training) has improved – potentially suggesting a causal link, but also an irony that more and more control is exerted as quality improves. Importantly, although teaching is a long-established profession, it means that it is not one that owns its standards of entry or development and is therefore subject to the whims of political policy and public funding. While this is to the detriment of creating a robust, independent profession that relies on evidence and impact to judge efficacy, there is much that school leaders can do to navigate policy change creatively and to reimagine professional development in their schools. By looking through the lenses of professional identity, progression and the future, and considering the role of schools in enabling collective agency, professional development policy can be refocused on teacher retention both at school level and, ultimately, in national policy thinking.

TEACHING AS A PROFESSION

Teaching can surely be considered to be among the oldest of professions, which is both a blessing and a curse. There is a widespread understanding of what it means to be a teacher stretching back thousands of years and, although lots of jobs may include elements of teaching, if somebody introduces themselves as a teacher to you at a party you can safely assume they are qualified to work in a school of some kind. But, despite this long historical recognition, it is only comparatively recently that teaching has developed some of the key hallmarks of any profession: the establishment of agreed standards of entry and ongoing development. More profoundly, these standards are not owned by the profession itself but rather have been developed and owned by the state, with consequences for how teachers are expected to perform and held to account, often driven by political and financial considerations more than evidence of efficacy. Choices about professional development have long been deliberately constrained by the decisions made in Whitehall rather than led by the judgement of individual teachers or school leaders. Over time this has meant a narrower and more controlled development experience for teachers that – whatever benefits may have accrued – has served to undermine the professionalism of teachers rather than enhance it.

Government interest in the performance of teachers stretches back to the early Victorian era and the pattern of governmental engagement in education was very different to that in, say, health: in education, governments tended to interest themselves directly in classroom practice, seeking a measurable return on investment, whereas in health, the focus was on public health policy (clean air and water) rather than directly in hospital and surgery practice (Ellis and Conyard, 2024). Nonetheless, although there were some government-sponsored programmes to support the training and development of teachers, it was not until after the Second World War that teachers were required, by the government, to have a qualification to teach. Prior to that, despite a mixture of sector-led and government initiatives, many teachers (especially in secondary schools) had no formal teaching qualifications. The decision to employ somebody was down to the school alone, based on whatever criteria they deemed appropriate. That changed with the wave of reforms sparked by public policy thinking during the Second World War, first with the McNair Report, published in May 1944, which sought to create more coherent structures and expectations of teacher training, and then with the decision by the Attlee government in 1946 to require that maintained schools used only qualified teachers (Board of Education, 1944).

It is worth pausing to reflect on the fact that the establishment of agreed standards of entry to the profession – that is the right to teach in maintained schools – was owned by the government rather than by the profession. That may have felt like a moot point in the post-war years as the emerging pattern meant governments left unions and teacher-training institutions to determine content of training and support classroom practice, but it did establish a clear precedent that regulation of professional identity came from Whitehall rather than from the profession (unlike other comparable professions such as medicine, accountancy, etc.).

In the decades following the end of the war, the main issue was to ensure an adequate supply of teachers as school-leaving ages were raised and more children completed a comprehensive education. Successive governments supported this work by funding teacher-training institutions which, although linked to universities, did not bestow a degree-level qualification on successful candidates, but rather a certificate to practice. The national focus was on the quantity of teachers needed to staff the system and the quality of teacher training was left to those working in teacher-training colleges to develop.

The mood music began to change in the 1960s as successive governments started to take an interest in what was happening in schools in much more detail. The reasons are complex, but included a recognition by ministers of the changing needs of the British economy, away from an industrial power where the labour market needed relatively few who were well qualified, to a technological power where education became more important in more roles; jobs requiring no qualifications sharply declined in number (Ellis and Conyard, 2024). Education became an issue of national economic need, so government interest in the quality provided by the maintained sector increased.

That interest, by successive governments, culminated most famously in the so-called Ruskin Speech delivered by then Prime Minister, Jim Callaghan, in 1976 when he said, 'Public interest is strong and legitimate and will be satisfied. We spend £6bn a year on education, so there will be discussion' (Callaghan, 1976). This work led to the 1977 Education in Schools Green Paper which set the context for potential reforms with a typically understated piece of civil service language:

> After a period of great and rapid changes in the size and character of the school population, accompanied by continuing reorganisation of the schools system, it would be surprising if there were not some degree of 'mismatch' between the needs of the schools and the capacity of the present teaching force to meet them.
>
> (DES and WO, 1977, p. 25)

In other words, the needs of the country and wider demographic changes meant that the government needed to be less focused on staffing (to reduce class sizes as a measure of quality) and could shift to thinking about the detail of teacher capability.

Among the many areas highlighted as needing attention, some of which still resonate today, were included:

- addressing concerns about whether entrants to teacher-training colleges were sufficiently literate or numerate;
- whether teaching training gave students sufficient subject knowledge or equipped them to manage classrooms;
- the lack of adequate induction for new teachers;
- the lack of any meaningful in-service training;
- recruitment gaps in subjects (such as maths, physics and design technology).

This was a seminal moment for the teaching profession. A political consensus was now firmly established that the government had no choice but to engage more directly to ensure the quality of teaching led to the student outcomes the economy demanded. There were, of course, political nuances: Conservative politicians tended to focus more on what are often referred to as traditional teaching methods, inspired by the so-called Black Papers of the late 1960s and early 1970s (Gillard, 1998), whereas Labour politicians tended to be more sympathetic to more progressive teaching methods, epitomised in the Plowden Report (Central Advisory Council for Education (England), 1967).

But any political differences were more noise than substance and we can see a clear continuity of thinking between the major parties on the regulation, control, performance management and accountability of the teaching profession. The work of Shirley Williams in the 1977 Education in Schools Green Paper (DES and WO) laid the groundwork for the Thatcher government to make teaching a graduate-entry only profession from 1979 onwards, and the Conservative government's 1983 Teaching Quality White Paper (DES and WO) used similar language to justify reforms to initial teacher education:

> initial teacher training courses are not always sufficiently closely geared to the needs of the schools; and some teachers are asked to undertake teaching programmes in parts of the curriculum for which the specialist elements of their education and training have not prepared them.
>
> (DES and WO, 1983, p. 2)

In 1988, in another example of the Conservatives taking forward a Labour idea, the then Secretary of State for Education, Kenneth Baker, introduced the five INSET days we still have (as suggested in the 1977 Education in Schools Green Paper (DES and WO)).

Throughout the subsequent decades we have seen multiple attempts by Labour, Conservative and coalition governments to review and improve initial teacher education content, to monitor delivery providers (including via Ofsted) and to use a mixture of coercion (making something mandatory) and cajoling (offering funding incentives) to ensure that teachers undertake the preferred training and professional development regime. Most recently, we can see that in the creation of the mandatory induction phase set out in the Early Career Framework (ECF) – responding to another issue raised in the 1977 Education in Schools Green Paper (DES and WO) – and funding for the so-called golden thread of national professional qualifications (NPQs), both of which have government-created frameworks, delivered by government-procured providers, who in turn are inspected by Ofsted to ensure they are delivering the ECF and NPQs with fidelity. In addition, the DfE funded a number of specialist hubs (covering maths, literacy and behaviour) to promote what it determines to be best practice, again selected by the department both in terms of content and who is permitted to deliver it. Such approaches inevitably lead to a lack of nuance and contextualisation at a school level, and are often driven by what the department can get the Treasury to fund rather than clear evidence of need or effect. That is not to say there is no engagement with the sector as plans are developed – both the ECF and NPQs were supported by expert groups for example – but it is carefully controlled through the selection of members and the parameters given to expert groups, and final decisions rest firmly with the government.

Against this backdrop, school leaders still maintain considerable autonomy in theory. They are still in the box seat when it comes to deciding what INSET should cover, and they are able to spend school budgets on other professional development for their staff. In practice, that autonomy is constrained by the expectations set out by Ofsted and the DfE (not without good cause, for example in terms of safeguarding requirements), and crucially by available funding. For example, between 2016 and 2023 the amount spent on professional development fell by 50 per cent in real terms in primary schools and 30 per cent in real terms in secondary schools (Teacher Development Trust, 2024a).

The net result is that, over the last half-century, the level of government prescription over the training and development of teachers has increased at the expense of professional autonomy. This seems to be fuelled by a basic distrust of the teaching profession. We can see it in the pseudo-academic ravings of Szamuely in the second Black Paper (1969) when he said:

> [The progressives'] whole campaign is now concentrated on a single issue: the use of education as a means of breaking down the country's social structure and creating 'equality of opportunity' – which is expected to lead inexorably to an egalitarian, possibly even 'classless' society. The Fifth Monarchy men have taken over from the educationists … Strangely enough, many of these latter-day egalitarians are also enthusiastic exponents of the 'permissive society'. We are, it seems, to be permissive in everything except education: in that field, and that field alone, the stern diktat of an enlightened-despotic state is to rule unchallenged. How they

manage to reconcile two such incompatible faiths is beyond my comprehension – but then so is most of the jumbled heap of twitching emotions that passes for the 'progressive' creed.

(Szamuely, 1969, p. 48)

And we can see it in the simpler, but no less damning use of the phrase 'The Blob' (in reference to ideological clashes with teachers and civil servants) made famous by former Secretary of State for Education, Michael Gove. Underpinning both is the notion that the teaching profession is unable to take responsibility for creating and maintaining high standards.

While we cannot accept that the state is a benign actor in this space, it is important that the teaching profession also considers its own complicity in accepting the oversight of government and its own failures to respond to the needs of the moment and take the initiative in raising standards. The motivations of unions, educational associations, schools and teachers themselves have not always been positive and a general approach of fighting against any form of performance management, lesson observation, or oversight within the system is as much a dereliction of professional responsibility as excessive government control is an undermining of professional agency. Indeed, it could be argued that given the lack of clear direction around standards by the profession, successive governments have had little choice but to be more interventionist to create greater consistency across the country and respond to extreme examples of systemic educational failures.

ENACTING POLICY: THE ROLE OF SCHOOL LEADERS

How, then, should the profession take responsibility for itself and its development, and what is its role in the policies that shape it? As Stephen Ball helpfully puts it (2017, p. 11):

> Policy action is almost always about reform, about doing things differently, about change and improvement ... Reform [since the 1970s] is not just about changing the way things are organised or done; it is about changing teachers and learning ... It is about rethinking, or 'reimagining' education and what it means to be educated – and this meaning is contested.

Part of a school leader's role is to implement government policies, but it may be more helpful to think of this as *enacting* policy: 'a process of re-interpretation and re-contextualisation in which policy actors work creatively in divergent ways' (Mincu et al., 2024, p. 1). Leaders understand that there are policies that must be 'done', but by bringing to the fore their moral purposes and values, they develop ways to enact policy that fits with their principles and furthers the direction that they have set for their school. This is going to become increasingly important as new government initiatives (around curriculum and assessment,

SEND and accountability, for example) need to be contextualised for pupils and teachers with different levels of expertise and understanding.

As we have seen, increasing government control over teachers' professional development has led to a narrower conception of what it means to teach, more control over the evidence that is deemed important and indeed a limiting of the institutions that are deemed 'suitable' to create and teach that evidence. This has had a profound and positive effect on teachers' skills and knowledge, providing a firm basis and a clear focus for new teachers in particular. It has also led to a greater codification of the evidence-base, and better understanding of teaching as an evidence-led profession – all of which has contributed to a reimagining of teacher professionalism. Unfortunately, it has not led to a profession that people are clamouring to join.

Instead, evidence-led practice, and the professional development that underpins it, is too often portrayed in policy as 'the best way of teaching all students'. It neither allows for teacher agency to interpret and apply the evidence in their own classrooms, nor for the idea that there may be other evidence, outside the prescribed canon, that could be useful. In particular, it does not consider that teachers could develop their own practice-based evidence which could challenge or extend the evidence-base. The narrow concept of 'fidelity' can easily lead to a perception that teachers are delivering someone else's agenda, and that there must be something wrong with them if the methods they're using don't work. This can't help but impact on teachers' self-efficacy and, ultimately, on their desire to stay in the job.

There is also increasing evidence of the role of school culture, and the leader's role in building culture and setting direction, on teacher professional development and, through that, on pupil outcomes (Kraft and Papay, 2014). And while it can be difficult to measure exactly how leadership makes the difference, research does show that leadership matters (see, for example, Robinson and Gray, 2019).

How then could we reimagine teacher education and, in particular, professional development, maintaining the vision of teaching as a profession with a strong evidence-base, but encouraging the development of professional voice and agency? What could professional development look like if it were focused on teacher retention? We suggest three different ways of looking at professional development: through the lenses of teacher identity, progression and the future.

PROFESSIONAL DEVELOPMENT AND TEACHER IDENTITY

Teacher identity, according to Judyth Sachs, 'provides a framework for teachers to construct their own ideas of "how to be", "how to act" and "how to understand" their work and their place in society' (Sachs, 2003, p. 135), while learning is 'a process of becoming' (Sachs, 2003,

p. 31). Importantly, teacher identity is developed collaboratively. In your school, what kinds of teachers are you growing through your professional development culture and your engagement with policy?

As we have seen, government policy can have the effect of pushing teachers towards compliance, particularly when training is part of a package of change. For example, the push towards synthetic phonics was accompanied by funded resources, national testing and accountability measures, making it very easy to comply. Compliance can happen for the best of reasons, that evidence is well-tested and is deemed to be the best that we currently have. It is important, particularly for beginning teachers, that they understand and use the practices based on this evidence. But if it places consistency or fidelity above the legitimate questions of teachers, it can lead to stagnation. It can also lead to schools which leap to fulfil each new policy and framework, sometimes even before those are finalised. In a system where government and its agencies review, consult and report at dizzying speed, a focus on compliance will lead very quickly to burnout.

A research-focused culture can begin from the evidence-base developed through the golden thread of the ECF. Teachers learn about the evidence, apply it in their classrooms and reflect – with a good mentor – on its success or otherwise. But if it stops there, or worse, it makes teachers feel that any 'failures' are their own rather than (perhaps) stemming from a need to revisit the evidence, it is in danger of becoming a different form of compliance culture. It also perpetuates the notion that professional development is a purely individual endeavour. Developing teachers who are confident to engage with research require more than individual reflection; they need opportunities to identify common themes across practice, to understand whether there are particular subjects or groups of students where the evidence seems less secure. As Elizabeth Atkinson argues, the purpose of research shouldn't just be to provide answers, 'but to inform discussion among practitioners, researchers and policymakers about the nature, purpose and content of the educational enterprise' (cited in Sachs, 2003, p. 89).

And this kind of discussion is at the heart of what Sachs calls the *activist professional identity*, which is underpinned by the principles of equity and social justice. This shouldn't be confused with political or union activism. Instead, it is about taking the debate about learning beyond research-focused discussions between professionals and fostering dialogue with the public. It is about both building professional expertise and making it visible and clearer to colleagues and others. Activist professionals collaborate to build a transformative vision of the future, working with academics, parents, policy-makers and each other to challenge assumptions, understanding and respecting difference, and privileging the perspectives of those who are most disadvantaged by the current system. A culture that empowers activist professionals puts practitioner research centre stage and gives time to explore learning and celebrate successes. It needs leaders who are confident, together, to reimagine policy in their particular contexts.

PROFESSIONAL DEVELOPMENT FOR PROGRESSION

Another way to consider professional development for retention is to think about progression opportunities. Much government-led professional development policy is based on the idea that teachers will progress from ITT through the ECF and into some form of leadership. But not every teacher wishes to move into leadership. We have identified two different forms of progression that may be helpful to consider: *career* and *learning*.

Career progression, as with learning and development, does not have to be linear. There are many roles that teachers can undertake which enable them to share expertise, but not necessarily to move into formal leadership roles. Some larger trusts are able to offer flexible opportunities outside the classroom, sometimes called *squiggle and stay*, which can support those returning after maternity leave or others who wish to work a little more flexibly. These could include providing support across different phases or subjects or working as ECT facilitators or mentors. There could also be opportunities for research or CPD leads, to support others while growing expertise in different areas. Some countries have developed different career structures to recognise the need for career progression. For example, Singapore has three different career tracks: alongside a 'school leadership' track, there is a 'teaching' track for those who wish to become 'master teachers' and develop other teachers' capabilities; and a 'senior specialist' track for those who want to specialise and break new ground (Ministry of Education Singapore, n.d.). As Lucy Crehan explores in *Clever Lands* (Crehan, 2016, p. 139), qualified teachers must choose one of those three tracks if they are to qualify for a pay rise after the first three years. There are professional development opportunities to match, and an array of teacher networks, many of which are set up and run by master teachers themselves. Of course, it helps that teachers in Singapore have less teaching time than those in England, and therefore more time for learning together.

It may also be helpful to consider progression as less about developing a professional career and more about growing professional learning. In work for the Scottish government, Menter et al. set out four paradigms of teacher professionalism which are ordered in terms of increasing degrees of agency. These are: the *effective* teacher, the *reflective* teacher, the *enquiring* teacher and the *transformative* teacher (Menter et al., 2010, p. 21). The effective teacher is the most politically driven model, focused on standards and compliance; the reflective teacher model is built on the importance of personal professional development, and opportunities for teachers to learn in the classroom, using research and collaborating with colleagues; the enquiring teacher model encourages teachers to undertake their own systematic enquiry in their classrooms, developing their practice and sharing their insights; the transformative model builds on the latter two and is closely related to Sachs' activist professionalism. They conclude by suggesting that the future of teacher professionalism should focus on teachers as both users and producers of knowledge, with 'increased control over the professional knowledge base of teaching' (Menter et al., 2010, p. 25). Each of these models may encourage leaders to reflect on their own professional development culture.

PROFESSIONAL DEVELOPMENT FOR THE FUTURE

Of course, school leaders must prioritise professional development around current concerns, both national and school-based. It is a truism that the quality of education cannot exceed the quality of its teachers, and it is right that CPD is focused on ensuring that pupils are taught by the most effective teachers. Teacher policy can – as we've seen in the development of training around the primary national strategies, for example – be linked extremely closely with pupil outcomes. This can lead to a perception that all opportunities are dictated from elsewhere and focused on giving information or building skills to use immediately. It can also shift the balance too far towards one-size-fits-all CPD.

In order to retain teachers, it is important that they have the skills and knowledge for the job. This, in large part, is the thinking behind the ECF. But what would policy on professional development look like if we considered more closely its impact on the future of the profession? We could look at this in two different ways: future conceptualisations of what it means to be a teacher, and how professionalism itself might change.

THE FUTURE OF TEACHING

The Teacher Development Trust is clear that 'Professional development should not just become part of what teachers do, but part of what being a teacher is' (TDT, 2024b, p. 6). For various reasons, CPD is still often seen as an add-on, courses to be taken in your own time, experts who come in with their PowerPoint™ slides. Even when it is developed as an opportunity to reflect on your classroom or leadership practice – through NPQs or the ECT, for example – it can end up as an additional burden on top of an overfull workload. We need to rethink teaching as going beyond the important work of teaching pupils, and the attendant planning, assessment, reporting, safeguarding and pastoral work that supports it. Engagement with research, mutual practising and learning with colleagues, even discussing, trialling and influencing government policies, need to be part of teachers' working lives beyond the early career period.

As we have seen from the Singapore model, time away from the classroom is essential so that professional development can be part of the day job, but equally teachers need opportunities to observe and be observed, to plan and teach together. This kind of 'lesson study' is key to professional development in Japan (Crehan, 2016, p. 96), and very different to the more judgemental lesson observations more prevalent in England. INSET days could be used in part for the kinds of professional development we have in mind, mutual engagement with research, classroom evidence and policy to improve practice in school.

Professional development also needs to be built into individual teacher performance management conversations and into timetabling for shared planning and team teaching. This both depends on and reinforces a culture of professional trust and learning.

THE FUTURE OF PROFESSIONALISM

The definition of professionalism developed by the Chartered College of Teaching includes within its three domains the recognition of teacher expertise, and bodies of knowledge that acknowledge multiple voices and perspectives; balancing commitment to their pupils with a focus on teachers' own wellbeing; and the importance of self-regulation and the professional ownership of standards (Müller and Cook, 2024). These, it argues, will lead to a profession with authority, esteem, status and prestige. It can be superficially easy to see these as things that are granted from outside the profession rather than grown from within.

For all its talk of resetting the relationship with teachers, the Labour government is unlikely to give up its control of schooling any time soon. Education plays such a vital role in the care of young children, the development of skilled workers and citizens, the creation of a better economy, society and planet that a strong role for government will always be important. If the profession is to take responsibility for creating and maintaining high standards, then we must work proactively to meet the needs of today and to build trust in our expertise.

Importantly, 'The moral purpose in schools as organisations coincides with the personal, which means a commitment to support the flourishing of all those involved, students and teachers alike' (Mincu et al., 2024, p. 11). For leaders, developing professionalism and trust is part of ethical leadership (ASCL, 2019). In particular, leaders must act courageously in the best interests of children and young people, even if that means challenging some forms of compliance culture. They use experience, knowledge and insight to develop excellent education that will change the world for the better, which includes supporting staff to challenge conventional wisdom and build new knowledge. They are open and honest in the decisions they make, and willing to change their minds if the evidence is strong. This should be true as much for political and policy leaders as it is for school leaders.

CONCLUSION

Not every teacher wants to be a researcher, but every teacher should approach evidence-informed practices with curiosity and a willingness to ask questions. Much of the evidence that underpins current practice is well-reviewed and trialled, but there is always the danger of snake oil sellers peddling easy and unfounded practices. Which of today's practices will become the 'learning styles' of tomorrow? Professional development in schools must encourage and provide frameworks for questioning the evidence, evaluating implementation and making changes as necessary. School cultures should enable all staff to speak out about misunderstandings and 'failures', whether they are experienced or newly qualified, in the majority or a lone voice. Mincu et al. speak of successful school leaders who 'deeply and gradually restructure the internal culture and processes while achieving a collective sense of belonging, agency, and commitment' (2024, p. 5).

Within schools, professional development policy could be reimagined to include individual expectations within performance management, and departmental, whole-school or beyond-school opportunities to share practice and reflections. It could provide structure for progression, from novice teacher to expert – remembering that teachers can become 'novice' each time they take on a new role – or more formally with the development of CPD or research leads, and routes into mentoring. Time could be set aside specifically for building pedagogical evidence together, with structured support for planning and teaching in teams, observing different practices and sharing reflections. A CPD 'menu' could be developed, so that teachers have more choice. To mitigate workload implications, a collaborative approach to understanding what teachers want, what expertise they have that they can share and what unnecessary work could be left undone will help to build cultures of trust and respect. There is, of course, no single answer and the context of schools and staff matter, but there is a strong evidence-base for the efficacy of the sorts of interventions suggested here (Timperley et al., 2007).

There are broader issues to be solved within the system, of course. Locally – through local authorities, multi-academy trusts (MATs) and Diocesan Boards for example – links need to be built with organisations that encourage research engagement, including universities, subject and professional associations, but also with employers, academic institutes, management and leadership experts. These could also be organisations that offer mentoring, peer review and supervision. Nationally, government needs to ensure that professional development policy is developed alongside reviews of curriculum, assessment and accountability rather than being an afterthought. In the longer term, a clear professional development policy is needed that considers career pathways linked with professional development, and opportunities to step out of the classroom in order to return – via traditional sabbaticals, externships or more creatively through engagement in community work or different employment with structured opportunities to reflect on its impact on teaching. These policies need to be developed from within the profession, with a government that is willing to listen and structures that enable teachers and leaders to engage in policy-making.

FURTHER LEARNING

- Sachs J. (2003) *The Activist Teaching Profession*. London: Open University Press.

  An exploration of teacher professionalism and how it can be developed and renewed through engagement with research, ethical practices and partnerships. It highlights the importance of inclusiveness, collaboration, passion and fun, and is a call to action to transform education.

- Kraft M.A. and Papay J.P. (2014) Can professional environments in schools promote teacher development? Explaining heterogeneity in returns to teaching experience. *Educational Evaluation and Policy Analysis* 36(4): 476–500.

  A seminal research paper that shows the importance not just of investing in professional development, but also in doing it within a supportive and considered culture in order to maximise returns on investment.

- Ellis N. and Conyard G. (2024) *Improving Education Policy Together: How It's Made, Implemented, and Can Be Done Better.* London: Routledge.

  An exploration of education policy-making in England, drawing out the history and influences on policy-makers, considering different ways of making policy from around the world and across the UK. It offers a framework for making policy collaboratively, iteratively and for the long term.

REFERENCES

Association of School and College Leaders (ASCL) (2019) *Framework for Ethical Leadership in Education.* Available at: www.ascl.org.uk/ASCL/media/ASCL/Our%20view/Campaigns/Framework-for-Ethical-Leadership-in-Education.pdf (accessed: 1 April 2025).

Ball, S.J. (2017) *The Education Debate.* London: Policy Press.

Board of Education (1944) *Teachers and Youth Leaders (McNair Report).* Available at: www.education-uk.org/documents/mcnair/ (accessed: 1 April 2025).

Callaghan, J. (1976) *A Rational Debate Based on the Facts.* Ruskin College Oxford, 18 October. Available at: https://education-uk.org/documents/speeches/1976ruskin (accessed: 1 April 2025).

Central Advisory Council for Education (England) (1967) *Children and their Primary Schools.* Plowden Report. London: HMSO. Available at: https://education-uk.org/documents/plowden/plowden1967-1.html (accessed: 24 April 2025).

Crehan, L. (2016) *Clever Lands: The Secrets Behind the Success of the World's Education Superpowers.* London: Unbound.

Department of Education and Science and Welsh Office (DES and WO) (1977) *Education in Schools: A Consultative Document.* London: HMSO. Available at: www.education-uk.org/documents/official-papers/1977-gp-education-in-schools.html (accessed: 1 April 2025).

DES and WO (1983) *Teaching Quality*. London: HMSO. Available at: www.education-uk.org/documents/official-papers/1983-wp-teaching-quality.html (accessed: 1 April 2025).

Ellis, N. and Conyard, G. (2024) *Improving Education Policy Together: How It's Made, Implemented, and Can Be Done Better*. London: Routledge.

Gillard, D. (1998) *Education in the UK: A History*. Chapter 12. Available at: www.education-uk.org/history/chapter12.html (accessed: 1 April 2025).

Kraft, M.A. and Papay, J.P. (2014). Can professional environments in schools promote teacher development? Explaining heterogeneity in returns to teaching experience. *Educational Evaluation and Policy Analysis*, 36(4), 476–500.

Menter, I., Hulme, M., Elliot, D. and Lewin, J., with Baumfield, V., Britton, A., Carroll, M., Livingston, K., McCulloch, M., McQueen, I., Patrick, F. and Townsend, T. (2010) *Literature Review of Teacher Education for the 21st Century*. Glasgow: Scottish Government. Available at: www.gov.scot/binaries/content/documents/govscot/publications/research-and-analysis/2010/10/literature-review-teacher-education-21st-century/documents/0105011-pdf/0105011-pdf/govscot%253Adocument/0105011.pdf (accessed 1 April 2025).

Mincu, M., Colman, A., Day, C. and Gu, Q. (2024) Lessons from two decades of research about successful school leadership in England: a humanistic approach. *Education Sciences*, 14(2), 187. Available at: https://doi.org/10.3390/educsci14020187 (accessed: 1 April 2025).

Ministry of Education Singapore (n.d.) *Professional Development*. Available at: www.moe.gov.sg/careers/become-teachers/pri-sec-jc-ci/professional-development (accessed 1 April 2025).

Müller, L.-M. and Cook, V. (2024) Revisiting the notion of teacher professionalism: a working paper. London: Chartered College of Teaching. Available at: https://chartered.college/wp-content/uploads/2024/05/Professionalism-report_2-May.pdf (accessed: 1 April 2025).

Robinson, V. and Gray, E. (2019) What difference does school leadership make to student outcomes? *Journal of the Royal Society of New Zealand*, 49(2), 171–87.

Sachs, J. (2003) *The Activist Teaching Profession*. London: Open University Press.

Szamuely, T. (1969) Comprehensive inequality. *Critical Survey*, 4(3), 48–56. Available at: www.jstor.org/stable/41553804 (accessed: 1 April 2025).

Teacher Development Trust (2024a) *SchoolDash Data: CPD Spending*. Available at: https://tdtrust.org/2024/06/07/schooldash-data-cpd-spending/ (accessed: 1 April 2025).

Teacher Development Trust (2024b) *Creating a CPD Entitlement That Works: Our Findings*. Available at: https://tdtrust.org/2024/02/29/creating-a-cpd-entitlement-that-works-our-findings (accessed: 1 April 2025).

Timperley, H., Wilson, A., Barrar, H. and Fung, I. (2007) *Teacher Professional Learning and Development: Best Evidence Synthesis Iteration (BES)*. Wellington, New Zealand: Ministry of Education.

2

TEACHER PROFESSIONALISM

THE IMPORTANCE OF PROFESSIONAL IDENTITY AND AUTONOMY FOR RETENTION AND CAREER PROGRESSION

DR VICTORIA COOK AND DR LISA-MARIA MÜLLER

INTRODUCTION

Amid an erosion of trust in and respect for our profession, a focus on developing and sustaining teacher professionalism must lie at the heart of efforts to address the current crisis in teacher recruitment and retention (Müller and Cook, 2024). Continuing professional development (CPD) has a pivotal role to play in raising the status of the profession, with evidence suggesting that it may help to improve rates of teacher recruitment and retention (Cordingley and Crisp, 2020).

The aim of this chapter is to introduce the Chartered College of Teaching's model of teacher professionalism, highlighting the central role of CPD and exploring its links with teacher professional identity and autonomy. In the second part of the chapter, we draw on two different examples of CPD to exemplify their possible impact on teacher professional identity and autonomy. Firstly, we draw on research that suggests personalised approaches to CPD can support the career progression of mid-career teachers who may not wish to move into leadership. Secondly, we demonstrate how journal clubs, a collaborative approach to CPD, may develop both individual and collective autonomy. Finally, we discuss the importance of critically examining both the content and the purposes to which CPD is being put, cautioning that collaboration does not always indicate a high level of autonomy or professionalism.

TEACHER PROFESSIONALISM

As the professional body for teachers, the mission of the Chartered College is to empower a knowledgeable and respected teaching profession. Adapting Mezza's (2022) conceptual framework of professionalism (Figure 2.1), we have redefined what we mean by teacher professionalism as part of our work to advocate for a more aspirational vision for our profession (Müller and Cook, 2024).

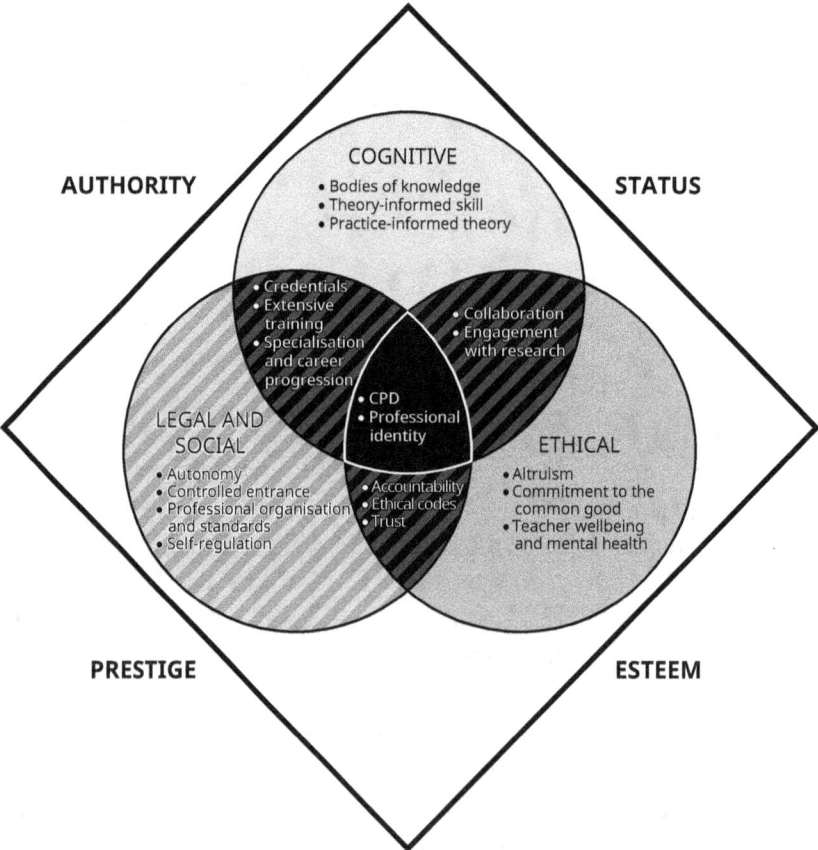

Figure 2.1 Working definition of professionalism, adapted from Mezza (2022) (Müller and Cook, 2024)

The notion of *teacher professionalism* is highly contested and is continually changing (Hargreaves, 2000). Our work is situated within Sachs' (2003) definition of *new* professionalism, which assigns teachers a more active role in policy-making, activism and the regulation of their own profession. We believe that this is vital if we are to attract and retain the best teachers to the profession. Mezza's (2022) original framework encompasses cognitive, legal/social and ethical domains presented in a Venn diagram. Explaining the rationale behind mapping these domains in this way, Mezza notes that this is designed to emphasise their interconnections and the role of contextual factors.

Our adaptation of Mezza's framework includes the addition of the concept of *practice-informed theory* in the cognitive domain, recognising teacher expertise as an essential aspect of evidence-informed practice. Practice-informed theory values teachers' role in adapting and implementing research evidence and building new knowledge from observations and action research. We also include the use of plural 'bodies' of knowledge, rather than the singular 'body of knowledge', within this domain to capture the multiplicity of voices that should be included as teachers engage with a wide range of evidence, acknowledging that there is no one-size-fits-all approach to teaching and learning. In the ethical domain, we believe the inclusion of teacher wellbeing and mental health is vital if teaching is to be a sustainable career choice. Improving wellbeing and reducing workload must be a key focus for policy-makers engaging in genuine partnership with the profession. Finally, we have relocated authority, prestige, esteem and status to sit outside the Venn diagram, viewing these as outcomes of the mechanisms described within the model. Thus, we argue, it is only by addressing the features of professionalism within the cognitive, ethical and legal and social domains that we may seek to raise the status of teaching to become a prestigious, highly esteemed profession where teachers have the authority to shape decisions that influence their professional lives.

Take, for example, teacher professional identity, which sits at the intersection of the three domains. The professional identity of teachers may be defined 'as a collection of beliefs, emotions and perspectives of themselves and their role as teachers, which is in constant development, depends on the context and varies between individuals' (Suarez and McGrath, 2022, pp. 8–9). Standing at the heart of the teaching profession, Sachs (2005) argues that teacher professional identity 'provides a framework for teachers to construct their own ideas of "how to be", "how to act" and "how to understand" their work and their place in society' (p. 15). Sachs notes that teacher identity is not fixed or imposed, but negotiated through experience and the understanding of that experience. Operating at the individual and collective level, teacher professional identity is influenced by a myriad of factors, including phase, subject, personal educational experiences and structures such as CPD, professional relationships and affiliations, mentor support and collaboration (Suarez and McGrath, 2022). As Suarez and McGrath argue, teacher identity is important for retention, helping to counteract some of the negative outcomes associated with increasing pressures from the education system.

Likewise, increased professional autonomy can function as a buffer against top-down decision-making (Demirkasimoğlu, 2010). Situated in the legal and social domain, the erosion of autonomy in the profession may be exemplified by the recent policy focus on evidence-informed practice. A top-down approach to evidence-informed practice risks constraining professional autonomy if research is communicated to teachers without considering the importance of context and professional judgement. Teachers require autonomy in interpreting and applying evidence to their contexts. As Scutt (2019) outlines, evidence-informed practice requires the careful combination of the best available research evidence with context-specific implementation and teacher experience, expertise and professional judgement (Figure 2.2).

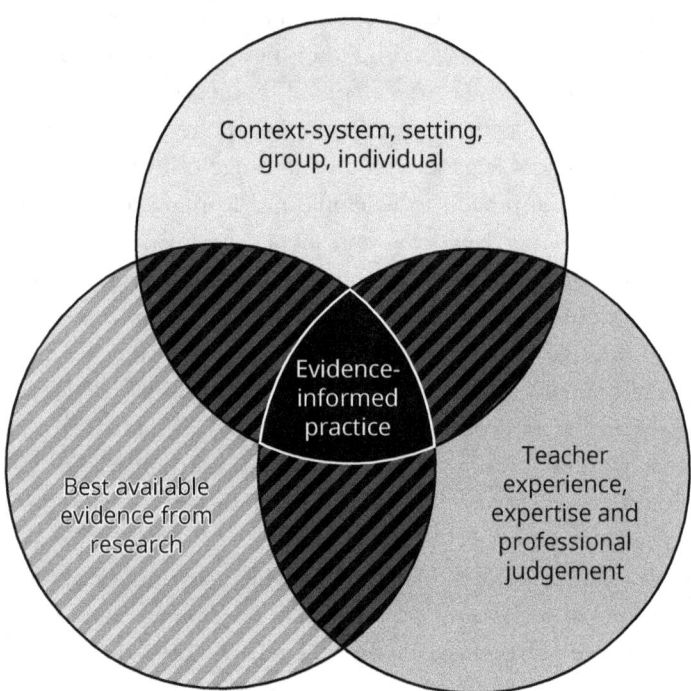

Figure 2.2 Evidence-informed practice (Scutt, 2019)

However, teacher autonomy is a complex concept. It is a multidimensional, layered and contextually sensitive phenomenon (Frostenson, 2015; Ingersoll, 2003; Wermke and Höstfält, 2014; Wermke et al., 2019), mediated by situated, professional, material and external factors (Keddie et al., 2024). It is therefore also important to consider what *types* of autonomy are indicative of authentic or meaningful professionalism.

Frostenson (2015, p. 24) distinguishes between 'general professional autonomy', 'collegial professional autonomy' and 'individual professional autonomy' (see also Day, 2020). General professional autonomy refers to the systems of governance and education reforms that shape teachers' work. Collegial autonomy relates to teachers' collective decision-making capacity to influence school-level organisational and pedagogical practices. Individual autonomy relates to the professional practice of the individual teacher and includes an individual's decision-making capacity over teaching materials, pedagogical approaches and the temporal and spatial conditions of work. Tensions may exist between these different dimensions of teacher professional autonomy, which in turn may be mediated by broader conditions of accountability in different times and spaces (Holloway and Parcerisa, 2024).

CPD sits at the heart of our understanding of teacher professionalism and, as such, has a pivotal role to play in raising the status of the profession. The next section explores some of the ways in which CPD may impact both teacher professional identity and autonomy.

RAISING THE STATUS OF THE PROFESSION THROUGH CPD

Our joint research project with colleagues from Sheffield Hallam University and Education Policy Institute on the professional development needs and experiences of mid-career teachers found that this was a heterogeneous group with differing and changing aspirations for their careers (Booth et al., 2021; Müller et al., 2021). This is supported by recent research mapping teacher professional development profiles in early-, mid- and late-career groups, which showed more diversity within career phases than between them (Coppe et al., 2024). While we found no agreed definition of mid-career teacher in our literature review, teachers appear to enter their mid-career after around five years in the profession. This broadly aligned with the findings from our survey of 88 teachers in England who self-identified as mid-career teachers. The survey findings also suggested that traditional school and subject leadership routes are not necessarily attractive options for this group, who often wish to be regarded as expert classroom practitioners rather than moving into managerial roles. As a result, the professional development needs of this group were frequently experienced as unmet. This lack of relevant professional development opportunities was found to potentially impact both retention and career progression. A majority of respondents (57 per cent) said that more targeted and tailored CPD opportunities would encourage them to stay in the profession, while 53 per cent reported that the CPD they participated in was not relevant for the next step in their careers. These findings indicate the need for more targeted, flexible CPD opportunities for mid-career teachers, including opportunities for professional learning outside leadership development. CPD opportunities that allow teachers to develop and be recognised for their classroom expertise, such as the Chartered College's Certificate in Evidence-Informed Practice and programmes by the Teacher Development Trust, may help to meet this need.

Journal clubs are another approach to CPD that can allow teachers to develop their classroom expertise. Journal clubs, which can operate at trust level, school level or departmental level, are a regular cycle of meetings that encourage practitioners to experiment with, and critically reflect on, new approaches that are rooted in evidence. Originally used in medical education (Linzer, 1987), more recently the model has been adapted for use in schools (Maxwell et al., 2022; Sims et al., 2017; Tallman, 2014; Tallman and Feldman, 2016). Journal clubs support practitioners to critically evaluate a range of different types of research evidence, both quantitative and qualitative, and consider how the findings may be translated into practice in their contexts. Many of the mechanisms for effective CPD are evident in the journal club model, including providing access to high-quality research, opportunities for peer learning, a clear link to practise and taking place over an extended period of time (Sims et al., 2021; Cirkony et al., 2021). Evidence from medicine suggests that journal clubs help to develop participants' knowledge and critical appraisal skills (Deenadayalan et al., 2008; Honey and Baker, 2011), which is supported through research on journal clubs in schools (Maxwell et al., 2022). In their evaluation of online journal clubs for science teachers run by the Chartered College of Teaching, Maxwell and colleagues identify statistically significant improvements on outcome measures related to confidence in accessing, assessing the quality of and applying research. Qualitative evidence further illustrates how, using tools developed as part of this programme, participants were supported to examine the validity, trustworthiness and relevance of research and apply research findings in a context-specific way.

In the section that follows, we provide a detailed analysis of a case study of a journal club in one secondary school to exemplify how the structures and practices of journal clubs can empower both individual and collegial forms of professional autonomy. This case study is drawn from a larger project conducted by the Chartered College of Teaching (April 2023 to April 2024), funded by the Fair Education Alliance, which sought to explore how journal clubs impact both teachers and teaching assistants (TAs) when supporting students with special educational needs and disabilities (SEND).

CASE STUDY: DEVELOPING INDIVIDUAL AND COLLECTIVE AUTONOMY THROUGH JOURNAL CLUBS

This case study is drawn from a non-selective mixed academy in the West of England with a cohort of approximately 1,000 students aged 11–16 years old. The school caters for a range of needs, with the number of students eligible for free school meals and students with a diagnosed SEND far exceeding the national average.

In this school, the journal club consisted of ten participants (three teachers and seven TAs). All participants completed journal club training online prior to starting the course. One teacher completed specific training to enable them to assume the role of journal club facilitator, who is responsible for guiding the discussion.

In the first journal club meeting, the participants discussed a piece of research exploring how students with SEND perceive and experience retrieval practice in mathematics (Gear, 2022). Gear's qualitative research with Year 5 (9–10 years) students found that they experienced retrieval practice as a *high stakes* test, which was in contrast to the assumed view of retrieval practice as a *low stakes* strategy. This led the journal club participants to discuss the language around retrieval practice and whether this could be causing anxiety for students with SEND in their setting. Despite the fact that the original research was carried out in a primary setting, the participants drew on their own professional experiences in their classrooms to reflect on the relevance of these findings for their students:

> **Higher-level TA**: *I don't think that it's necessarily different in terms of the kids. I think that it applies equally to our kids with quizzing and feeling anxious around these tests. I mean, we see that all the time. A student last year we had to remove from lessons for every quiz and test because she was so anxious about them. Anyways, I think in terms of identity around particularly maths and quizzing is quite strong across all age groups really.*

The participants then discussed their ideas for how they could adapt their practice in light of the research findings. In the four weeks between the first and second meetings, participants were encouraged to implement a change to their practice in light of these discussions. In the second meeting, participants were asked to critically reflect on the changes that they had made:

> **Science teacher**: *So, the first thing, the use of language and terminology and when we say the words 'assessment' and 'test' it can have often quite negative connotations with the students. And we talked about trying to rephrase it. So we have to use the phrase 'interim assessment' […] with a Year 9 class interim assessment, and when we said that it again caused some anxiety. But we sat there and rephrased it as a check-in, a topic check-in, it did help actually reduce the anxiety about what we were trying to do.*

This extract exemplifies how the teacher exercised their decision-making power over the approach to retrieval practice used in their classroom, deliberately altering the language associated with this strategy to help reduce students' anxiety. Several other participants exercised their individual autonomy in similar, but subtly different, ways as they altered

(Continued)

teaching materials and approaches to retrieval practice in response to the specific needs of their students in their classrooms. Such was the success of these changes that the journal club participants discussed the importance of cascading their findings to the whole school, and how they might go about doing this:

> **Higher-level teaching assistant**: *[I]t's worth a few bullet points I think in a bulletin about ways to alleviate test anxiety.*
>
> **Facilitator**: *Or even the SENCO briefing, from our SENDCO.*
>
> **Special educational needs coordinator**: *I go to Heads of Faculty meetings now. I write in their newsletters sometimes. But Heads of Faculty has been a really good way for me to get messages across because then they take those to their teams.*

Here we see the journal club participants exercising their collective decision-making capacity to influence pedagogical practices enacted at the school level. By creating a safe space in which participants were supported to critically interpret research and use their professional judgement to apply this to their contexts, the journal club thus empowered both individual and collegial autonomy. By empowering practitioners in this way, these findings suggest that journal clubs support teachers to shape their ongoing professional work, which is central to the development of a strong professional identity.

However, collaboration does not always indicate a high level of autonomy or professionalism. Holloway and Parcerisa (2024) outline how the mandated curriculum framework in Victoria (Australia) requires teachers to collaborate, which works against autonomy and professional discretion. They argue that, by forcing teachers to interact with one another, teachers become subjects of administrative control rather than participants of an authentic and spontaneous collaborative culture, creating what Hargreaves and Dawe (1990) called *contrived collegiality* (see also Hargreaves, 2019):

> Collaborative cultures comprise evolutionary relationships of openness, trust, and support among teachers where they define and develop their own purposes as a community. Contrived collegiality consists of administratively contrived interactions among teachers where they meet and

> work to implement the curricula and instructional strategies developed by others. Collaborative cultures foster teacher and curriculum development. Contrived collegiality enhances administrative control.
>
> (Hargreaves and Dawe, 1990, p. 227)
>
> Journal clubs enable participants to define and develop their own purposes as a community, choosing what articles to discuss and how to implement what they have learned (Tallman, 2014; Sims et al., 2017). In this way, individual and collegial autonomy is organic, rather than contrived.

CONCLUSION

CPD is an important tool for empowering teachers with individual and collegial autonomy and developing professional identity. Professional identity and autonomy are both important for the development of teacher professionalism. If teaching is to develop into a prestigious, highly esteemed profession where practitioners want to stay and progress, teachers must be provided with high-quality and relevant CPD opportunities, where the development of classroom expertise is appropriately recognised and rewarded as an alternative to traditional routes into leadership. It is also vital that practitioners are encouraged to critically engage with research evidence and given the autonomy to make the best decisions for their students. However, CPD is not a silver bullet for raising the status of the teaching profession: it is important to critically examine both the content and the purposes to which CPD is being put.

These findings have important implications for the different ways in which teacher professionalism may be nurtured in schools. By enabling teachers to take greater responsibility for their own CPD throughout different career stages and exploring new types of collaboration we seek to empower teachers to shape decisions that influence their professional lives, thus acknowledging the complexity of teachers' working lives.

FURTHER LEARNING

- Müller L.M. and Cook V. (2024) *Revisiting the notion of teacher professionalism: a working paper.* London: Chartered College of Teaching. Available at: https://chartered.college/wp-content/uploads/2024/05/Professionalism-report_2-May.pdf (accessed 1 April 2025).

    This report explores the meaning of teacher professionalism and why it is important for the profession.

- Chartered College of Teaching (nd) An introduction to journal clubs. Available at: https://my.chartered.college/facilitating-effective-journal-clubs (accessed 4 August 2025).

  This bitesize learning unit from the Chartered College of Teaching gives you the opportunity to reflect on how journal clubs might be used to support evidence-informed practice in your context.

- Education Endowment Foundation (2021) Effective Professional Development. Available at: https://educationendowmentfoundation.org.uk/education-evidence/guidance-reports/effective-professional-development (accessed 4 August 2025).

  This EEF guidance supports schools in selecting external CPD and designing and delivering their own CPD.

REFERENCES

Booth, J., Coldwell, M., Müller, L.M., Perry, E. and Zuccollo, J. (2021) Mid-career teachers: a mixed methods scoping study of professional development, career progression and retention. *Education Sciences*, 11(6), 299.

Cirkony, C., Rickinson, M., Walsh, L., Gleeson, J., Salisbury, M., Cutler, B., Berry, M. and Smith, K. (2021) Beyond effective approaches: a rapid review response to designing professional learning. *Professional Development in Education*, 50(1), 24–45. https://doi.org/10.1080/19415257.2021.1973075

Coppe, T., Parmentier, M., Kelchtermans, G., Raemdonck, I., März, V. and Colognesi, S. (2024) Beyond traditional narratives about teacher professional development: a critical perspective on teachers' working life. *Teaching and Teacher Education*, 139, Article 104446. https://doi.org/10.1016/j.tate.2023.104436

Cordingley, P. and Crisp, B. (2020) Professional learning and recruitment and retention: what global regions can tell us. In T. Ovenden-Hope and R. Passy (eds), *Exploring Teacher Recruitment and Retention: Contextual Challenges from International Perspectives*. Oxford: Routledge, pp. 131–47.

Day, C. (2020) How teachers' individual autonomy may hinder students' academic progress and attainment: professionalism in practice. *British Educational Research Journal*, 46(1), 247–64. https://doi.org/10.1002/berj.3577

Deenadayalan, Y., Grimmer-Somers, K., Prior, M. and Kumar, S. (2008) How to run an effective journal club: a systematic review. *Journal of Evaluation in Clinical Practice*, 14, 898–911.

Demirkasımoğlu, N. (2010) Defining 'teacher professionalism' from different perspectives. *Procedia-Social and Behavioral Sciences*, 9, 2047–51.

Frostenson, M. (2015) Three forms of professional autonomy: de-professionalisation of teachers in a new light. *Nordic Journal of Studies in Educational Policy*, 1(2), 1–15.

Gear, R. (2022) How do children with special educational needs experience retrieval practice? *Impact*, 16 (September). Available at: https://my.chartered.college/impact/issue-16-autumn-2022/ (accessed: 13 January 2025).

Hargreaves, A. (2000) Four ages of professionalism and professional learning. *Teachers and Teaching: History and Practice*, 6(2), 151–82.

Hargreaves, A. (2019) Teacher collaboration: 30 years of research on its nature, forms, limitations and effects. *Teachers and Teaching*, 25(5), 603–21. https://doi.org/10.1080/13540602.2019.1639499

Hargreaves, A. and Dawe, R. (1990) Paths of professional development: contrived collegiality, collaborative culture, and the case of peer coaching. *Teaching and Teacher Education*, 6(3), 227–41.

Holloway, J. and Parcerisa, L. (2024) Teacher collaboration: how conditions of accountability shape teachers' autonomy, responsibilities, and relationships. *Teachers and Teaching*, 31(1), 1–15. doi: 10.1080/13540602.2024.2436028

Honey, C.P. and Baker, J.A. (2011) Exploring the impact of journal clubs: a systematic review. *Nurse Education Today*, 31(8), 825–31.

Ingersoll, R.M. (2003) *Who Controls Teachers' Work? Power and Accountability in America's Schools*. Cambridge, MA: Harvard University Press.

Keddie, A., MacDonald, K., Blackmore, J. and Gobby, B. (2024) Teacher professional autonomy in an atypical government school: matters of relationality and context. *Oxford Review of Education*, 50(3), 434–49. doi: 10.1080/03054985.2023.2236941

Linzer, M. (1987) The journal club and medical education: over one hundred years of unrecorded history. *Postgraduate Medical Journal*, 63(740), 475–8. https://doi.org/10.1136/pgmj.63.740.475

Maxwell, B., Booth, J., Bevins, S., Halliday, J., Hotham, E., Nelson, J., Lucas, M. and Andrade, J. (2022) Supporting science teachers to engage with and carry out research. Project Report. Sheffield Hallam University.

Mezza, A. (2022) *Reinforcing and Innovating Teacher Professionalism: Learning from Other Professions*. OECD Education Working Papers No. 276. Paris: OECD.

Müller, L.-M. and Cook, V. (2024) Revisiting the notion of teacher professionalism: a working paper. London: Chartered College of Teaching. Available at: https://chartered.college/wp-content/uploads/2024/05/Professionalism-report_2-May.pdf (accessed: 1 April 2025).

Müller, L.M., Booth, J., Coldwell, M., Perry, E. and Zuccollo, J. (2021) Continuous professional development and career progression in mid-career teachers. *Impact*, 11, 13–16.

Sachs, J. (2003) *The Activist Teaching Profession*. London: Open University Press.

Sachs, J. (2005) Teacher education and the development of professional identity: learning to be a teacher. In P.M. Denicolo and M. Kompf (eds), *Connecting Policy and Practice: Challenges for Teaching and Learning in Schools and Universities*. London: Routledge, pp. 5–21.

Scutt, C. (2019) Is engaging with and in research a worthwhile investment for teachers? In C. Carden (ed.), *Primary Teaching*. London: Sage, pp. 595–610.

Sims, S., Fletcher-Wood, H., O'Mara-Eves, A., Cottingham, S., Stansfield, C., Van Herwegen, J. and Anders, J. (2021) *What are the Characteristics of Teacher Professional Development that Increase Pupil Achievement? A Systematic Review and Meta-analysis*. London: Education Endowment Foundation.

Sims, S., Moss, G. and Marshall, E. (2017) Teacher journal clubs: how do they work and can they increase evidence-based practice? *Impact*, 1, 72–5.

Suarez, V. and McGrath, J. (2022) *Teacher Professional Identity: How to Develop and Support it in Times of Change*. OECD Education Working Papers 267. Paris: OECD. doi: 10.1787/b19f5af7-en

Tallman, K. (2014) A journal club: a scholarly community for preservice and inservice science teachers. PhD thesis, University of Massachusetts. doi: 10.7275/t0bg-6z12

Tallman, K.A. and Feldman, A. (2016) The use of journal clubs in science teacher education. *Journal of Science Teacher Education*, 27(3), 325–47. doi: 10.1007/s10972-016-9462-7

Wermke, W. and Höstfält, G. (2014) Contextualising teacher autonomy in time and space: a model for comparing various forms of governing the teaching profession. *Journal of Curriculum Studies*, 46(1), 58–80.

Wermke, W., Olason Rick, S. and Salokangas, M. (2019) Decision-making and control: perceived autonomy of teachers in Germany and Sweden. *Journal of Curriculum Studies*, 51(3), 306–25. doi: https://doi.org/10.1080/00220272.2018.1482960

3

THE CHALLENGES SCHOOLS FACE IN RECRUITING TEACHERS

ORGANISATIONAL CULTURES AND THE COMPLEXITY OF THE ITT MARKET

POLLY BUTTERFIELD-TRACEY

INTRODUCTION

England's education system faces an ongoing teacher shortage, with the Department for Education's (DfE) recruitment targets consistently missed and retention rates remaining low. This challenge is exacerbated by the complex and dynamic initial teacher training (ITT) market, characterised by provider consolidation, increased competition and a loss of local provision. Trainee teachers often navigate a confusing application process, experience pressure to accept offers and encounter a lack of flexibility and low morale within schools. School leaders face significant challenges in providing subject specialist mentors for trainees, providing adequate release time for mentor meetings and training, and managing the different programme requirements of the ITT providers they work with.

This chapter examines the multifaceted factors contributing to this crisis, with a particular focus on the complexities of the ITT market and the challenges school leaders face when recruiting teachers and engaging in ITT. It proposes a collaborative approach to address these challenges, offering practical strategies for school leaders to enhance teacher recruitment.

THE COMPLEX LANDSCAPE OF TEACHER RECRUITMENT AND RETENTION

England's schools are facing a growing challenge in securing adequate teacher supply. Despite increased demand for teachers, particularly in state-funded secondary schools, postgraduate ITT recruitment continues to fall below pre-pandemic levels. Moreover, the DfE's recruitment targets have been consistently missed, and early career teacher (ECT) attrition rates remain stubbornly high.

The persistent and growing shortfall of applications to ITT programmes in England, has coincided with a period of unprecedented change for the ITT sector. As part of the government's *Initial Teacher Training Market Review* (DfE, 2022) all providers of ITT had to undergo a rigorous re-accreditation process against a set of new quality requirements, including increased mentoring requirements and the introduction of intensive training and practice (ITAP) elements. The wording and structural recommendations within the *ITT Market Review* report seemed to prioritise large-scale providers with contracted 'delivery partners', rather than smaller school-based provision, which operates at a more local level with locally driven approaches to training. Following the accreditation process the market has been reconfigured significantly with a marked number of providers exiting the market or forming different partnerships, and large-scale national providers entering the market. This shift, alongside a shrinking pool of applicants, has led to an increasingly challenging environment in some localities, as smaller providers who lost their accreditation also lost their ability to design provision which is truly local and involves their partner schools in design and delivery.

School leaders report challenges in meeting the demands of different ITT providers, particularly around release time for mentors and employment-based trainees, and trainee teachers express that it is complex and confusing to navigate their way through application to training programmes, that they are subject to pressure to accept places offered (and reject others) and that, once they have begun to train, they frequently encounter low morale, high workload and barriers to flexible working in schools. The culture in schools, including workload expectations and teacher wellbeing, significantly impacts the attractiveness of the school as an employer and of teaching as a profession.

THE PERSISTENT TEACHER SHORTAGE

Last academic year, the DfE missed its target for secondary school teacher recruitment by 50 per cent (DfE, 2024a) and is almost certain to miss its teacher recruitment target again this year, despite slashing it by almost a tenth. Issues are pronounced in shortage subjects with 12 out of 17 subjects missed. At the time of writing, recruitment for secondary ITT courses for 2024–25 remains significantly below target again at 62 per cent (DfE, 2024b).

Alongside the challenges ITT providers face in recruiting trainees, many schools are also unable to recruit qualified teachers in shortage subjects and are increasingly having to accept teachers outside their subject specialism or employ unqualified teachers. A report by the House of Commons Education Committee found widespread use of non-specialist teachers in schools struggling with recruitment, with 62 per cent of such schools reporting some maths, physics and languages lessons being taught by non-specialists (House of Commons Education Committee, 2024). Deploying non-specialist or unqualified teachers is a key approach for mitigating shortages, most prevalent in schools struggling with recruitment and schools in disadvantaged areas (Worth and Faulkner-Ellis, 2022). This is despite concerns that recruiting non-specialist or unqualified teachers may have negative implications for teaching quality. While subject-specific bursaries, particularly for mathematics and science, have offered some mitigation, they have proven insufficient to address the ongoing teacher supply crisis.

A factor exacerbating the recruitment crisis is the high numbers of teachers leaving the profession each year. Last year the workforce grew by fewer than 300 teachers overall as the number leaving the profession continues to rise. The DfE workforce figures covering 2022/23 show that 39,971 teachers left state-funded teaching for reasons other than retirement – or 8.8 per cent of the workforce (DfE, 2024d). When it comes to ECTs, the figures show high numbers are still quitting early into their careers, despite the additional support and training they now receive through the two-year *Early Career Framework* (ECF). A total of 11.3 per cent quit in 2022/23 after just one year of teaching. This figure rises to 25.9 per cent after three years and 32.5 per cent after five years. Fewer than 60 per cent of teachers remain in the profession after ten years (House of Commons Education Committee, 2024).

While early career retention payments (ECRPs) for mathematics and physics teachers have shown promise in increasing retention within these STEM subjects (Sims and Benhenda, 2022), financial incentives alone are not sufficient to address the root causes of high teacher attrition. Non-financial factors, such as excessive workload and lack of flexible working, significantly influence teachers' decisions to enter and remain in the profession (DfE, 2019; Adams et al., 2023). A 2023 review of flexible working approaches by the Education Endowment Foundation (EEF) found that teachers with little possibility of accessing flexible working were more likely to say they planned to leave in two years or earlier (46 per cent), compared to teachers who could possibly or very likely access flexible working (35 per cent and 26 per cent respectively) (Harland et al., 2023). This led the authors to estimate that 'access to flexible working arrangements would have the equivalent impact on retention as a 4.34 per cent increase in annual pay' (Burge et al., 2021). Despite government efforts to reduce workload since the 2014 Workload Challenge (DfE, 2015), this remains a persistent hurdle.

NAVIGATING THE EVOLVING ITT LANDSCAPE

In the five years prior to the *ITT Market Review* (DfE, 2022) there was a 70 per cent increase in the number of ITT providers (DfE, 2014, 2019), with accredited school-based initial teacher training providers (SCITTs) almost doubling. The recommendations within the *ITT Market Review* report appeared to favour moving the sector towards a model which encouraged economies of scale, rather than localised provision, potentially risking teacher supply in hard-to-reach, disadvantaged and rural areas (Hollis, 2021). While the re-accreditation process streamlined the market (only 179 providers accredited, with 68 existing providers losing accreditation (DfE, 2022)), overall assessment by the NFER is that most de-accredited providers, especially the largest, have continued to deliver through new partnerships, such as the delivery partner model favoured within the report (Worth, 2023). So the sector continues to compete over a shrinking pool of applicants by employing a vast range of recruitment tactics, from targeting internal candidates in schools (especially TAs) to sponsorship of local sports teams, contacting armed forces, roadside advertising, and running their own events, campaigns and incentives (NASBTT, 2023). Since 2024, ITT providers have reported increasingly ruthless recruitment behaviours to sector meetings, and receive feedback from applicants that they are being pressured to accept places prior to completing all of their arranged interviews. The range of partners involved in ITT currently includes accredited providers who award qualified teacher status (QTS) (higher education institutions (HEIs), regional accredited SCITT providers or national providers), delivery partners such as multi-academy trusts (MATs), local alliances, teaching school hubs and ITT regional hubs. The result is a set of complex, dynamic and constantly changing inter-relationships.

This market can be challenging for school leaders, as working with multiple providers means meeting the demands of differing programme requirements. These demands include contrasting dates for placements and ITAP elements, inconsistency with central-based training days, mentor training and assignment deadlines. The challenge is increased for schools with trainees on employment-based routes, who must not only release trainees for one day of central-based training each week, but also manage the disruption caused by second school placements and the 20 ITAP days (which are in addition to school placements). While providers have tried to minimise the disruption to schools, the challenges for the employing school and for the employment-based trainees themselves remain. Increasingly schools or MATs are opting to work with just one accredited provider in order to minimise disruption for pupils and reduce the workload for the professional mentor. However, a potential consequence of this is a narrowing of provision, including training in smaller subjects and on specialist routes. Some MATs have become delivery partners for national providers, and the sector has reported an increase in local conflicts of interest and exclusive arrangements (Hollis, 2021). These arrangements potentially reduce opportunities for local collaboration and support and do little to increase the supply of trainee teachers to hard-to-reach and rural areas. This can limit the provision for these schools as well as the opportunities for trainees, such as spending time in schools serving disadvantaged communities, or a focused period teaching pupils from disadvantaged backgrounds. To be effective, this model requires national processes to be aligned with the strengths and needs of the local community and with school values (Cordingley et al., 2020). School leaders then, are expected to navigate this complex ITT system which asks them to align research-informed pedagogy, curriculum and local community needs.

The desire for flexible working is recognised as one of the main reasons why it is harder to recruit trainee teachers; however, it is challenging to offer due to the increase in delivery costs. Flexible working is challenging for schools, but more prevalent in the wider labour market since Covid, with 44 per cent of graduates now mainly working from home (NFER analysis of the DfE survey (DfE, 2024d)). The demand for flexible and part-time ITT programmes has also increased since the pandemic as trainees face considerable costs during their training year, including tuition fees, travel expenses and living costs, so for many it is necessary to work part time alongside training. This is particularly true for parents of young children and career-changers; around half of teachers with parental responsibilities report requesting flexible working to help them manage parental responsibilities while working (Hollis, 2021; Adams et al., 2023). Such a factor is particularly important as career-changers are one of the few areas of growth in ITT recruitment (applications from the over 40s are up 38 per cent compared to 2023 (Now Teach, 2024)). While the number of flexible and part-time programmes has increased for the current recruitment cycle, providers report challenges with schools unwilling to offer part-time mentors due to timetabling constraints, or uncertainty about placement capacity beyond one academic year.

Despite the *ITT Market Review*'s stated aim of providing 'a more efficient and effective market' (DfE, 2022), potential applicants to ITT courses must still navigate many decision points when selecting their courses (fee-funded, employment-based); choose between funding options (apprenticeship, salaried, student finance, self-fund); select flexible, part-time or full-time provision; phase options (Early Years, 5–11, 7–14, 11–16, 11–18 and 14–19) and types of academic award (QTS, PGCE, PGDE, PGTA). This means that in reality there are dozens of different possible routes into teaching. Adding extra frustration for applicants is the time it takes for the confirmation of their placement school. We know from DfE research that applicants are most likely to make a choice about their ITT provider based on the geographical location of their placement; however, candidates are not always able to search by placement schools and are instead presented with hundreds of possible placement schools which may not be confirmed until the start of their ITT course. All of this is particularly challenging for those with young children, or those working part time to support themselves while training.

THE IMPACT OF SCHOOL CULTURE ON RECRUITMENT AND RETENTION

Beyond tangible factors like workload reduction and access to flexible working arrangements, school culture significantly influences teacher recruitment and retention. A positive school culture encompasses a range of factors, including strong leadership, a supportive and collaborative environment, clear communication channels and a focus on professional development.

The prevailing discourse surrounding education, coupled with the persistent quality and standards narrative within policy reform and the national media, significantly impacts teacher perceptions of and recruitment to the profession. This, combined with low teacher morale within staffrooms, can contribute to a negative perception of the profession and discourage potential candidates from entering (or remaining in) teaching. Trainees and ECTs frequently report the negative ways in which teaching is spoken about in school staffrooms and in the wider public community, and research confirms that teachers frequently feel the profession does not receive the respect it deserves. The most recent available Ofsted research into teacher wellbeing recommends that the DfE must spread the message that teaching is a highly valued and important occupation (Ofsted, 2019).

School culture is highlighted as an important non-financial factor affecting retention. Key findings from the OME *Teacher Retention* report (Burge et al., 2021) show that school culture (along with workload and teacher environment) is highly valued by teachers, so much so that teachers would be willing to trade off financial rewards to work in environments where they received support from school leadership and other teaching colleagues. A collaborative and supportive environment can also improve retention, as poor school culture was stated as the main reason for teachers planning to leave the profession. Ofsted's *Teacher Wellbeing at Work* report (Ofsted, 2019) also recommended that schools develop staff wellbeing by creating a positive and collegial working environment in which staff feel supported, valued and listened to. The report concluded that creating such an environment is one of the main ways in which we can improve wellbeing and enhance retention (Ofsted, 2019, p. 8).

Research indicates that flexible working arrangements can have a positive impact on teacher wellbeing and job satisfaction (Harland et al., 2023). The *Working Lives of Teachers and Leaders* survey (Adams et al., 2023) found that teachers who worked flexibly reported higher job satisfaction and felt their work–life balance was better considered by their managers compared to those without flexible arrangements. While barriers such as timetabling issues and unsupportive leadership may exist, these can be mitigated through careful logistical planning and the development of a whole-school culture that values and supports flexible working options. This requires a shift in mindset and a commitment from school leaders to recognise the benefits of flexible working for both teachers and the school itself (CooperGibson Research, 2020; Sharp et al., 2019).

Experiencing a positive school culture during their training placement can act as a powerful magnet for ECTs. Prospective teachers are drawn to schools with a reputation for strong leadership, supportive colleagues and a focus on teacher wellbeing. Schools that prioritise collaborative environments, offer arrangements for flexible working and cultivate a sense of community are more likely to attract and retain high-quality educators.

PRACTICAL STRATEGIES FOR SCHOOL LEADERS TO ENHANCE TEACHER RECRUITMENT BY ENGAGING IN ITT

School leaders face significant challenges recruiting teachers and engaging in ITT. The complex and evolving ITT market presents numerous hurdles, and navigating the demands of multiple providers, managing release time for mentors and trainees, and meeting the varying requirements of different programmes all place a burden on schools. Furthermore, the shrinking pool of applicants, coupled with challenging recruitment practices in some localities, creates a competitive environment that can hinder collaboration and support between all stakeholders. The desire for flexible training and working arrangements among trainee teachers further complicates the process, requiring schools to adapt their practices while navigating potential barriers to implementing these options.

To overcome these challenges, a collaborative approach is essential. By cultivating strong partnerships between schools, universities, local accredited ITT providers, Teaching School hubs, and other key stakeholders, we can leverage the collective expertise and resources within the education system and enable the development of innovative solutions to address the teacher shortage.

THE COLLABORATIVE APPROACH

Engaging in ITT presents schools with the opportunity to recruit ECTs and offer internal career progression for support staff to move into teaching. Wider partnerships further support the development of teachers beyond their early careers and into middle and senior leadership. A collaborative approach can enable schools to work seamlessly with a range of partners, and the aspiration should be that all those partners share a joined-up approach that addresses local issues through shared knowledge and experience, allowing partners to influence and inform each other's strategies and operational responses. Prioritising local needs and context is crucial for the success of this approach, ensuring that partnerships are responsive to the specific challenges and opportunities within the local education system. By valuing the contributions and expertise of all stakeholders, a more collaborative approach is possible to address the barriers to engaging in ITT and recruiting teachers. Through joint initiatives such as shared recruitment strategies, co-designed mentorship programmes, regional trainee pools and the development of flexible training pathways, a more supportive and sustainable system for teacher education can be created. While challenges present barriers to collaboration – such as existing dynamics and competition, the wider recruitment crisis and an ever-changing set of requirements and frameworks – the long-term benefits of building wider, meaningful relationships across the sector and the region are significant. These relationships can provide school leaders with the partnerships they need to recruit, retain and develop their staff.

There are three key types of organisations that schools can work with to develop partnerships:

- *teaching school hubs*: these are led by schools and trusts, acting as centres for teacher training and support. They offer professional development programmes for educators at all stages of their careers, including ITT, national professional qualifications and early career support;
- *accredited ITT providers*: only these organisations can deliver teacher training courses that lead to qualified teacher status through various routes, such as fee-funded programmes, employment-based training and assessment-only routes. Accredited providers include universities, local accredited school-based providers and national providers;
- *national subject hubs*: these hubs specialise in specific subjects (currently English, maths and music) and focus on developing expertise and sharing best practices in teaching these disciplines.

These partnerships provide schools with a range of training opportunities to support, develop and retain their staff.

SCENARIOS

SCENARIO A

An experienced TA in your primary school has the aspiration to become a teacher but does not hold an undergraduate degree.

Training option: TA to Teacher Apprenticeship pathway

A TA with aspirations to teach can pursue a TA to Teacher Apprenticeship pathway. If the TA holds a Level 3 or Level 5 TA Apprenticeship, their prior learning may be recognised towards a Level 6 Degree Apprenticeship, potentially reducing the duration of the degree programme. This pathway allows the TA to progress their career while contributing to the school. Upon completion of the degree, they can then undertake an employment-based ITT programme, leading to QTS while simultaneously filling a teaching vacancy within the school.

Partners involved in training:

- apprenticeship provider: Level 3 or 5 Teaching Assistant Apprenticeship;
- university partner: Level 6 Degree Apprenticeship or BA Primary;
- accredited SCITT provider: employment-based training route to the award of QTS.

SCENARIO B

A vacancy is likely to become available in your maths department that would be suitable for an ECT.

Potential solution: host a trainee for their B Placement with a view to making an early offer of employment, and offer to showcase your school as part of ITAP

To proactively address future staffing needs, schools can strategically engage in ITT by hosting a trainee for one of their school placements when a vacancy is anticipated within the department. This provides an excellent opportunity for the school to observe a potential ECT in action and build a relationship with the trainee. By offering employment to successful trainees, schools can ensure a smooth transition and provide the ECT with a supportive environment to begin their teaching career. Where subject knowledge enhancement is required, such as at KS5, schools can collaborate with local maths hubs to provide targeted support. When a suitable mentor is not available then consider working with ITT providers to showcase your school as part of their ITAP elements.

Partners involved in training:

- ITT provider (signposted by local teaching school hub);
- ECF programme provider;
- maths hub (for subject knowledge enhancement).

SCENARIO C

Year 3 teacher with potential for academic leadership.

Potential solution: mentoring and teacher development programmes

To retain and develop high-performing teachers, schools can invest in their professional growth even where progression opportunities are not readily available. Teachers with leadership potential can be supported through mentoring programmes for ITT and ECT, allowing them to develop valuable leadership skills and contribute to the professional development of other teachers. This experience can serve as a pathway for career progression into roles such as subject leader, phase leader, or assistant headteacher. Further opportunities for leadership development include participation in the National Professional Qualification for Leading Teacher Development (NPQLTD), often delivered through partnerships with national providers and local delivery partners.

Partners involved in training:

- local accredited ITT provider;
- ECT mentoring: teaching school hub or national provider;
- NPQLTD: national provider with local delivery partner.

SCENARIO D

You have an unqualified teacher working in your English department.

Training option: assessment-only (AO) route to qualified teacher status

As part of the government's new Wellbeing and Schools bill, from 2026 all teachers must have or be working towards QTS. If you have an experienced unqualified teacher with a degree working in your school, then the AO route can allow them to demonstrate that they already meet the Teachers' Standards, without the need for further training.

Partners involved in training:

- accredited ITT provider: assessment-only route to QTS.

RECOMMENDED STRATEGIES FOR SCHOOL LEADERS

1. *Build local strategic partnerships*:
    - *collaborate with teaching school hubs*: leverage their expertise to identify suitable local ITT providers who offer the subjects and age ranges your school needs, and to explore wider partnership opportunities;
    - *engage with subject hubs*: utilise the expertise and resources of the remaining national subject hubs (e.g. music, maths, English) to address specific subject shortages and enhance teacher development in your departments;

- *form strategic alliances*: collaborate with other local schools, successful MATs and local authorities to share resources, develop joint recruitment strategies and create trainee talent pools.

2. *Create an attractive employer culture*:
   - *showcase unique strengths*: collaborate with ITT providers to host elective opportunities for trainee teachers, or speak with the teaching school hub your school is assigned to find out about showcasing your school during ITAP elements;
   - *develop clear career pathways*: utilise the expertise across your collaboration to understand all available routes for professional development (e.g. TA to teacher, teacher to leader) and plan career pathways for staff at all levels;
   - *embrace flexible working and training*: explore and implement flexible working arrangements for teachers, consider hosting trainees on flexible routes to better understand how flexibility can be offered to qualified teachers. Explore flexible training routes for your staff by working with universities providing flexible degree courses.

3. *Optimise ITT engagement*:
   - *build strong relationships with local ITT providers*: involve yourself in interview, school experience days, elective visits and early placement requests to help secure a pool of high-quality trainees;
   - *address mentor challenges*: develop strategies to address mentor shortages, including offering release time and payment for mentoring duties, and exploring shared mentoring approaches with the help of your ITT provider;
   - *minimise disruption for employment-based trainees*: explore creative approaches to manage placements for employment-based trainees, including applying for reductions in placement duration, requesting flexibility in the timing of placements and organising trainee swaps to ensure consistent mentoring.

4. *Cultivate a collaborative approach*:
   - *share best practice*: engage in regular knowledge sharing and best practice sharing with other schools, ITT providers and stakeholders within the local education system;
   - *advocate for system-level change*: collaboratively advocate for policy changes and system improvements that support teacher recruitment and retention.

CONCLUSION

This chapter has explored the multifaceted challenges facing schools in recruiting and retaining teachers within the context of a complex and evolving ITT market. These challenges include a persistent teacher shortage, high attrition rates and the complexities of navigating the changing landscape of ITT provision. The chapter has highlighted the crucial role of school culture in attracting and retaining high-quality teachers, emphasising the importance of creating supportive and collaborative environments that prioritise teacher wellbeing and professional development. Furthermore, the chapter has emphasised the significance of a collaborative approach to address these challenges. By cultivating strong partnerships with ITT providers, teaching school hubs and other key stakeholders, schools can leverage collective expertise, share best practices and develop innovative solutions to address the teacher shortage. A collaborative approach enables schools to navigate the complexities of the ITT market, support trainee teachers effectively and create a more sustainable and rewarding teaching profession. School leaders are encouraged to actively participate in building these partnerships, advocate for system-level improvements and prioritise the creation of a positive and supportive school culture to ensure the long-term success of teacher recruitment and retention efforts.

FURTHER LEARNING

- GOV.UK (2024) Finding a teaching school hub. Available at: www.gov.uk/guidance/teaching-school-hubs (accessed 4 August 2025).

    Find a teaching school hub to get support with finding a local ITT provider and access professional development for your staff. Available at: www.gov.uk/guidance/teaching-school-hubs

- The National Association of School-Based Teacher Trainers (NASBTT) (2024) The Future of Initial Teacher Training – A Manifesto for Change. Available at: https://www.nasbtt.org.uk/the-future-of-initial-teacher-training-a-manifesto-for-change-2/ (accessed 4 August 2025).

    Read this 'manifesto for change', which outlines five solution-focused proposals to support the recruitment of teachers.

- Department for Education (2024) Initial Teacher Training and Early Career Framework (ITTECF). Available at: https:// assets.publishing.service.gov.uk/media/661d24ac08c3be25cfbd3e61/Initial_ Teacher_ Training_and_Early_Career_Framework.pdf (accessed 4 August 2025).

    Read the following explainer from *Schools Week* on the five key changes involved in developing the combined ITTECF: Cumiskey, L. (2024) *New Teacher Training Framework: Everything You Need to Know*. Available at: https://schoolsweek.co.uk/dfe-combines-two-flagship-schemes-into-new-initial-teacher-training-and-early-career-framework-after-ecf-review/ (accessed: 25 April 2025).

REFERENCES

Adams, L., Coburn-Crane, S., Sanders-Earley, A., Keeble, R., Harris, H., Taylor, J. and Taylor, B. (2023) *Working Lives of Teachers and Leaders: Wave 1*. London: DfE.

Burge, P., Lu, H. and Phillips, W. (2021) *Understanding Teacher Retention: Using a Discrete Choice Experiment to Measure Teacher Retention in England*. RR-A181-1. Cambridge: RAND Europe.

CooperGibson Research (2020) *Exploring Flexible Working Practice in Schools: Final Report*. Available at: https://assets.publishing.service.gov.uk/government/uploads/system/uploads/attachment_data/file/938537/Exploring_flexible_working_practice_in_schools_-_final_report.pdf (accessed: 25 April 2025).

Cordingley, P., Higgins, S., Greany, T., Crisp, B., Araviaki, E., Coe, R. and Johns, P. (2020) Developing great leadership of CPDL. CUREE, University of Durham and University of Nottingham.

DfE (2014) *Initial Teacher Training: Trainee Number Census – 2013 to 2014*. Available at: gov.uk/government/statistics/initial-teacher-training-trainee-number-census-2013-to-2014 (accessed: 16 May 2025).

DfE (2015) *Government Response to the Workload Challenge*. Available at: https://assets.publishing.service.gov.uk/government/uploads/system/uploads/attachment_data/file/415874/Government_Response_to_the_Workload_Challenge.pdf (accessed: 16 May 2025).

DfE (2019) *Initial Teacher Training (ITT) Census for 2019 to 2020, England*. Available at: gov.uk/government/statistics/initial-teacher-training-trainee-number-census-2019-to-2020 (accessed: 20 December 2024).

DfE (2022) *Initial Teacher Training (ITT) Market Review: Overview*. Available at: www.gov.uk/government/publications/initial-teacher-training-itt-market-review/initial-teacher-training-itt-market-review-overview (accessed: 25 April 2025).

DfE (2024a) *Initial Teacher Training Census: Academic Year 2023/24*. Available at: https://explore-education-statistics.service.gov.uk/find-statistics/initial-teacher-training-census/2023-24 (accessed: 20 December 2024).

DfE (2024b) *Initial Teacher Training Census: Academic Year 2024/25*. Available at: https://explore-education-statistics.service.gov.uk/find-statistics/initial-teacher-training-census/2024-25 (accessed: 30 January 2024)

DfE (2024c) *Schools, Pupils and their Characteristics: Academic Year 2023/24*. Available at: https://explore-education-statistics.service.gov.uk/find-statistics/school-pupils-and-their-characteristics/2023-24 (accessed: 5 January 2025).

DfE (2024d) *School Workforce in England: November 2023*. Available at: www.gov.uk/government/statistics/school-workforce-in-england-november-2023 (accessed: 5 January 2025).

Harland, J., Bradley, E. and Worth, J. (2023) *Understanding the Factors that Support the Recruitment and Retention of Teachers: Review of Flexible Working Approaches*. London: Education Endowment Foundation.

Hollis, E. (2021) *The Case for Smaller, Local Level School-Based ITT*. National Association of School-Based Initial Teacher Trainers (NASBTT). August. Northampton: NASBTT.

House of Commons Education Committee (2024) *Teacher Recruitment, Training and Retention*. May. Available at: https://committees.parliament.uk/publications/44798/documents/222606/default/ (accessed: 16 January 2025).

National Association of School-Based Initial Teacher Trainers (NASBTT) (2023) *ITT Recruitment Barriers to Delivery Survey*. May. Available at: https://s3.eu-west-2.amazonaws.com/media.nasbtt.org.uk/wp-content/uploads/2023/05/09091417/ITT-recruitment-and-barriers-to-delivery-survey-May-2023.pdf (accessed: 25 April 2025).

Now Teach (2024) *Open letter*. Available at: https://nowteachlive.b-cdn.net/live/media/eyyd2l2h/letter-of-support-letter.pdf (accessed: 16 May 2025).

Ofsted (2019) *Teacher Well-being at Work in Schools and Further Education Providers*. London: Ofsted, pp. 4–45.

Sharp, C., Smith, R., Worth, J. and Van den Brande, J. (2019) *Part-Time Teaching and Flexible Working in Secondary Schools*. National Foundation for Educational Research (NFER). Available at: www.nfer.ac.uk/publications/part-time-teaching-and-flexible-working-in-secondary-schools/ (accessed: 25 April 2025).

Sims, S. and Benhenda, A. (2022) The effect of financial incentives on the retention of shortage-subject teachers: evidence from England. Working paper No. 22-04. Available at: https://repec-cepeo.ucl.ac.uk/cepeow/cepeowp22-04.pdf (accessed: 16 May 2025).

Worth, J. (2023) *ITT Reforms Haven't Been Catastrophic – But Fears Remain*. NFER, 29 November. Available at: www.nfer.ac.uk/blogs/itt-reforms-haven-t-been-catastrophic-but-fears-remain/ (accessed: 16 May 2025).

Worth, J. and Faulkner-Ellis, H. (2022) *Teacher Supply and Shortages: The Implications of Teacher Supply Challenges for Schools and Pupils*. London: NFER.

4

UNDERSTANDING THE UNDER-REPRESENTATION OF MINORITY ETHNIC TEACHERS

BENG HUAT SEE, STEPHEN GORARD AND FUJIA YANG

INTRODUCTION

The aim of this chapter is to examine the challenges faced in increasing the ethnic diversity of the teaching workforce in England, and to understand the factors associated with these challenges. We begin with an overview of the patterns and trends in the ethnic disproportionality of teachers and pupils in England, and the leaking pipeline from student applications to teacher training to employment in school. We then examine the factors attracting teachers to a school, or encouraging them to leave, especially the role of school leaders. The evidence here is based on a national survey, analysis of school workforce census data (available via gov.uk for various years) and syntheses of international evidence.

BACKGROUND

With increasing migration, and a growing minority ethnic population in England, the lack of ethnic diversity in the teaching workforce has become a concern. While student cohorts are becoming more ethnically diverse, the same is not true for teachers. White British teachers make up 84 per cent of the workforce, while only 64 per cent of pupils are White British (gov.uk, 2021a, 2021b). Those from minority ethnic backgrounds account for 35 per cent of students, yet teachers from minority ethnic backgrounds represent only 15 per cent of the workforce.

This disproportionality or imbalance is even more pronounced in leadership roles, with 93 per cent of headteachers and 90 per cent of assistant headteachers being White British (Gorard et al., 2023a; gov.uk, 2021b). Disproportionality also varies across geographical regions. London, despite having the most diverse teacher workforce, has the highest disproportionality of any region of England due to an even greater mismatch between teacher–student demographics. Conversely, the North East has the lowest disproportionality despite having the lowest number of minority ethnic teachers, because the teacher and pupil populations are better aligned. However, this means that many minority ethnic students in that region would encounter a teacher or school of their own ethnicity, while White British students in those areas have limited exposure to authority figures from different backgrounds.

Such ethnic disproportionality is not unique to England. Similar disparities have been observed in other countries, including the US (US Department of Education, 2016; Blom et al., 2017; Lindsay, 2017; Ingersoll et al., 2019).

WHY DISPROPORTIONALITY MIGHT MATTER

The under-representation of minority ethnic teachers can have important implications for both students and the profession. International evidence suggests that a student lacking teachers of the same ethnic group might be treated differently at school. For example, minority ethnic students with teachers from similar ethnic backgrounds are less likely to be excluded (Grissom et al., 2009; Lindsay and Hart, 2017) or suspended from school (Wright, 2015) or to drop out (Gershenson et al., 2022). They are less likely to be seen as disruptive or inattentive (Dee, 2005) or classified as needing special education (Stiefel et al., 2022) and more likely to be referred to a gifted programme (Grissom and Redding, 2016; Grissom et al., 2017). Minority ethnic teachers tend to have slightly higher expectations of minority students than White teachers do (Gershenson et al., 2016).

However, much of the existing research focuses on the US context, particularly Black American and Hispanic students, who differ culturally from Black African and Black Caribbean students in the UK. The UK also has a significant South Asian population from Pakistan and Bangladesh, that is not prominent in the US. Moreover, these studies are largely correlational and often overlook factors like prior attainment and socio-economic background. This means the observed patterns may not be due to ethnic match or mismatch.

A more general argument for diversifying the teaching workforce is that schools serve as a microcosm of society and, therefore, should reflect the diversity of the wider society to which students belong. Exposure of teachers from various backgrounds prepares students for the multicultural world they will navigate beyond schools. All students can benefit from a diversity of cultural experiences and understanding. Having staff of minority ethnic heritage can help foster inclusivity and reduce segregation (Gorard and Smith, 2010; Gorard, 2018). This benefits all students and promotes social cohesion.

Ethnic disproportionality may also affect the wellbeing of minority teachers, who are more likely to work in under-resourced schools with high levels of disadvantaged pupils (Carver-Thomas, 2018; Ingersoll et al., 2017).

To address these disparities, policies across England (gov.uk, 2018), Wales (Welsh Government, 2023) and Scotland (Scottish Government, 2021) aim to increase ethnic diversity in teaching to create a closer match between the ethnicity of teachers, school leaders and their students. Tackling bias in the recruitment and promotion of school leaders can improve the retention and supply of minority teachers. Research shows that there is a strong link between minority school leaders and the hiring and retention of minority ethnic teachers (e.g. Bailes and Guthery, 2022; Bartanen and Grissom, 2019; Goff et al., 2018; See et al., 2024). Supportive leadership and a positive school culture are also crucial for improving working conditions and thus improving retention for all teachers.

This chapter first presents evidence of the increasing ethnic disproportionality in our teaching force, drawing data from the Department for Education (DfE), the University and Colleges Admissions Service (UCAS), the Organisation for Economic Co-operation and Development (Teaching and Learning International Survey) (OECD/TALIS) and the Office for National Statistics (ONS). It explores the reasons behind the under-representation of minority ethnic teachers and possible solutions, incorporating findings from a national survey of 3,646 teachers and an international review of research on improving diversity in education (Gorard et al., 2025).

GROWING ETHNIC DISPROPORTIONALITY IN THE TEACHING WORKFORCE

For each ethnic group, we calculated the ratio of teachers/deputy heads/heads to pupils in each year. Note that, in all comparisons, we are comparing the proportion of teachers from each ethnic group relative to the total number of teachers with the proportion of pupils from each ethnic group relative to the total number of pupils.

Between 2010 and 2021 the proportion of White British students fell from 80 per cent to 65 per cent, whereas the proportion of White British teachers declined by only 4 per cent from 89 per cent in 2010 to 85 per cent in 2021 (Figure 4.1). At the same time, the proportion of minority ethnic students increased from 23 per cent to 35 per cent (an increase of 12 percentage points) whereas the number of minority ethnic teachers grew by only 4 per cent from 11 per cent to 15 per cent). The rate of growth of minority ethnic teachers is far below that for students. This means that White British teachers remain over-represented in schools compared to White British pupils.

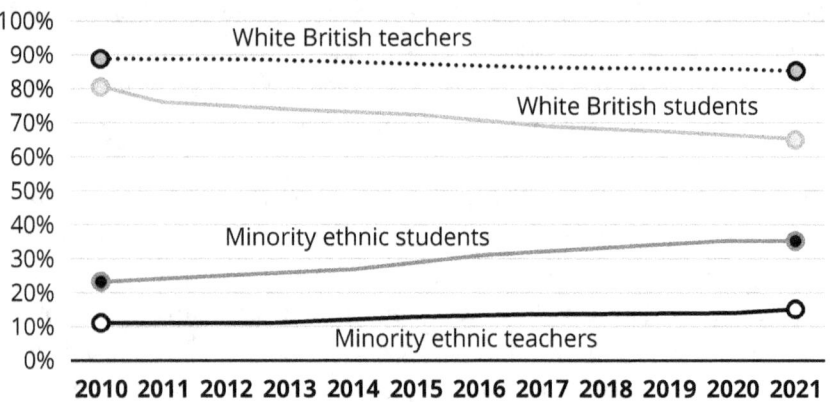

Figure 4.1 Trends in disproportionality between teacher and pupil population (2010 to 2021)

Looking at the proportion of teachers and pupils by ethnicity, data from the school workforce census show that White British teachers are consistently over-represented compared to White British pupils. In 2021, there were over 1.2 times more White British teachers than there were White pupils (Figure 4.2). Of all the ethnic groups, Black Caribbean is the only group where teacher numbers have approached parity with Black Caribbean pupils (0.78 to 1.03).

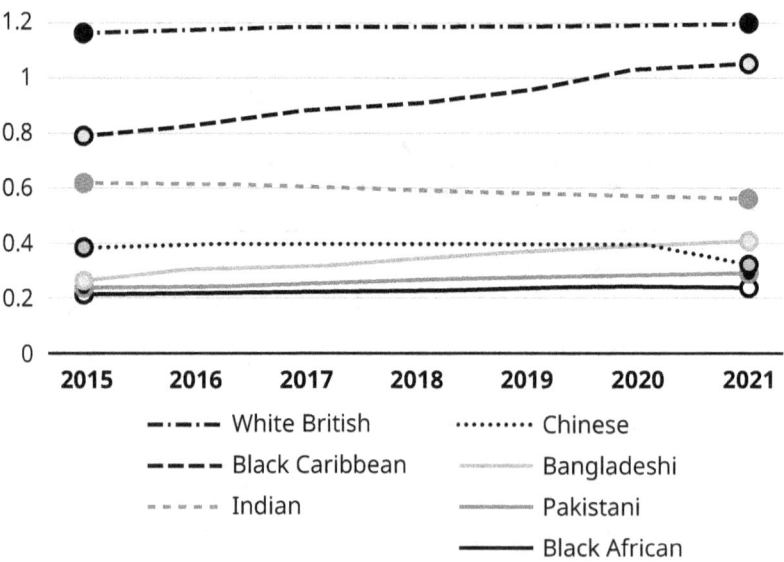

Figure 4.2 Trends in disproportionality of classroom teachers and pupils by ethnic group (2015 to 2021)

This is primarily because of a decline in the number of Black Caribbean pupils (Figure 4.3). Teachers from other ethnic groups, including Black African and the major groups of Asian teachers, remained significantly under-represented compared to pupils of the same ethnicity.

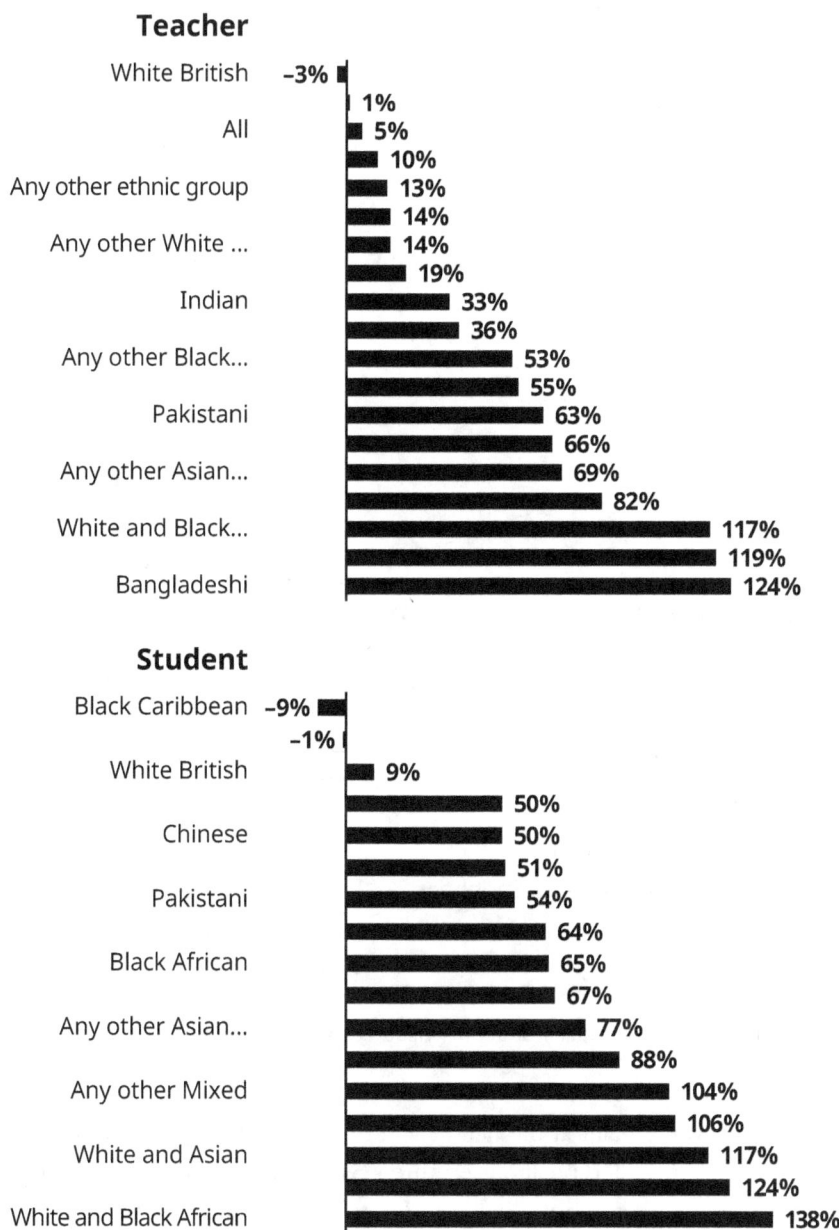

Figure 4.3 Change in teacher and student ethnic profile (2011 to 2021)

For ease of reading, we display only the main ethnic groups here. For more details, see Gorard et al. (2023a). Between 2011 and 2021, the numbers of Black African, Indian and Pakistani students have increased by more than 50 per cent. At the same time, the teacher population had also increased. The largest growth was among Bangladeshi teachers (124 per cent) followed by White and Black Caribbean (117 per cent), mixed ethnicities, Pakistani (63 per cent), other Black (53 per cent) and White and Black African (55 per cent). However, despite this rapid growth in teacher numbers, the proportion of Bangladeshi and Pakistani teachers is still below that of students of the same ethnicity, although there is a slight improvement for Bangladeshi teachers, where disproportionality has moved from 0.27 to 0.4.

The disproportionality is even more pronounced for promoted staff. Compared to the pupil population, there are over 1.3 times as many White British deputy heads as there are White British pupils (Figure 4.4).

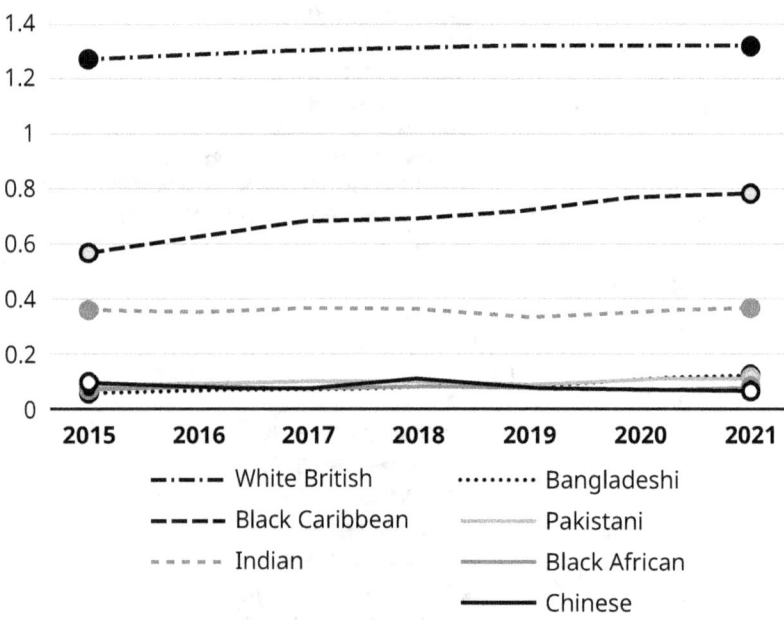

Figure 4.4 Trends in disproportionality of deputy headteachers and pupils, by minority ethnic group

The imbalance is even greater at the headteacher level. While the number of ME teachers has grown, few are in promoted positions (Figure 4.5). Despite some positive signs, progress is slow. For instance, the disproportionality index for Bangladeshi deputy heads improved from 0.06 in 2015 to 0.122 in 2021 – a step in the right direction, but significant disparities still exist. Minority ethnic pupils are already unlikely to have a teacher who shares a similar background, and the likelihood of seeing a minority ethnic role model in a position of school leadership is even more remote. The situation is particularly concerning for Black African, Pakistani, Bangladeshi and Chinese pupils, who are least likely to see someone of their ethnicity in a leadership role. This lack of representation could have profound implications for role models and aspirations.

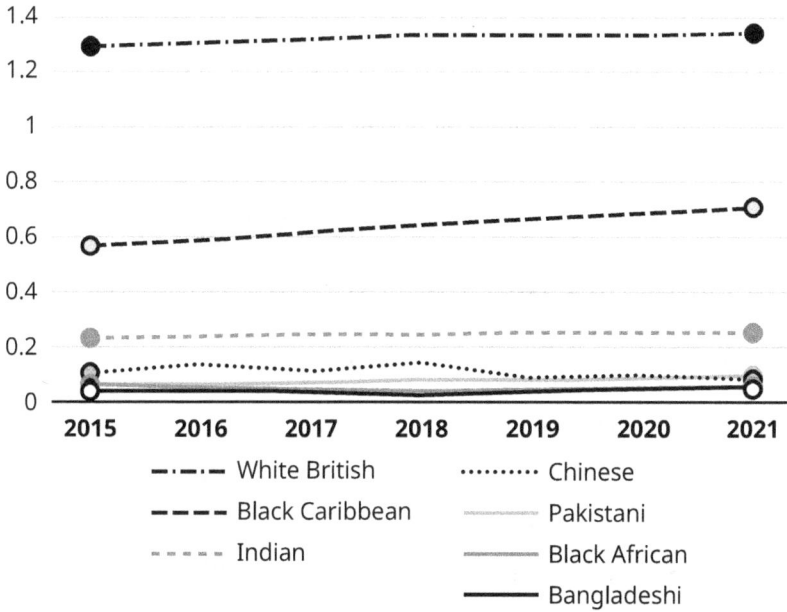

Figure 4.5 Trends in disproportionality of headteachers and pupils, by minority ethnic group

COMPARISON OF TEACHER–PUPIL ETHNIC DISPROPORTIONALITY BY REGION

Across most regions, the proportion of White teachers compared to the proportion of White pupils is between 1 and 1.2, indicating a close parity in the proportion of White teachers and White pupils (Figure 4.6). However, London is an exception, exhibiting the greatest disproportionality despite having the highest proportion of minority ethnic teachers. This is because of the much higher proportion of minority ethnic pupils. London has over twice as many White teachers compared to the proportion of White pupils, and this disproportionality is growing over time. In other regions – for example, the West Midlands where there is a relatively high proportion of minority ethnic pupils – there are slightly more White teachers than their pupil numbers would suggest.

56 TEACHER RECRUITMENT, RETENTION AND CAREER PROGRESSION

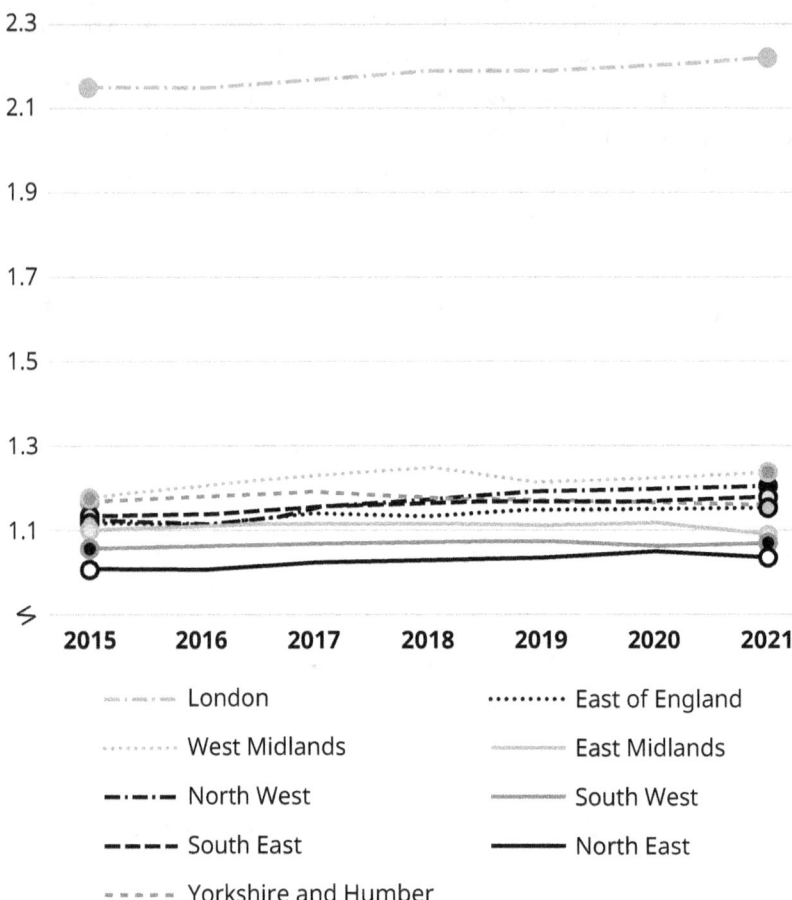

Figure 4.6 Trends in disproportionality of White British teachers to White British pupils, by region

CHALLENGES IN ADDRESSING THE DISPROPORTIONALITY GAP

Although the number of minority ethnic teachers has grown over time, White British teachers are still over-represented in many schools and at the leadership level. One way to close the gap is to increase the number of minority ethnic teachers significantly at a rate above the growth of the minority ethnic population.

The issue, however, is not the lack of individuals from minority ethnic background wanting to be teachers. Our research found that at every stage from application to training to employment at school, minority ethnic applicants are less likely to be successful. UCAS data show that there has been an increase in the number of minority ethnic teachers applying to

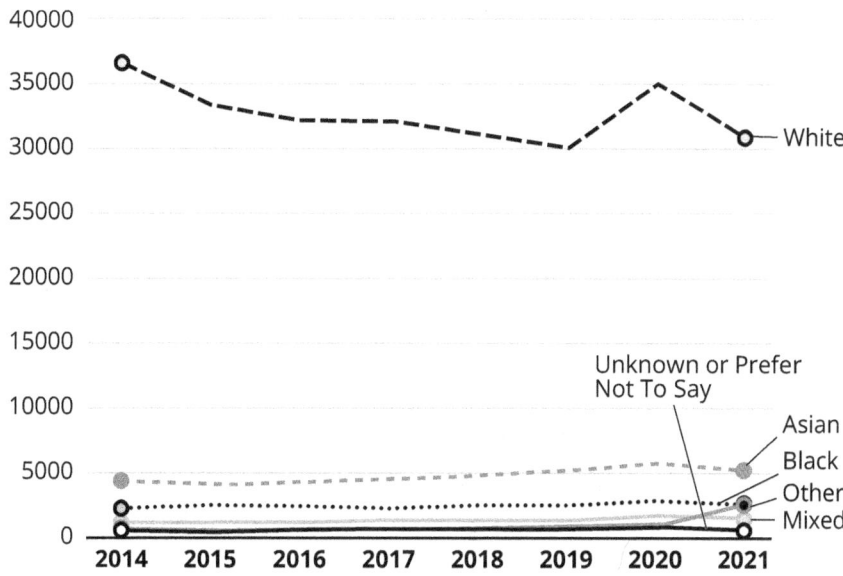

Figure 4.7 Number of applicants to initial teacher training by ethnicity (England)

Source: UCAS Teacher Training End of Cycle 2021 Data Resources. *Available at*: www.ucas.com/data-and-analysis/ucas-teacher-training-releases/ucas-teacher-training-end-cycle-2021-data-resources *(accessed: 25 April 2025)*

ITT, although the number of applicants for all groups has dropped in the last year shown (Figure 4.7). The group that made the biggest increase between 2014 and 2020 is Other (+72 per cent), followed by the Unknown (+62 per cent), Mixed ethnicity (+39 per cent), Asian (+35 per cent) and Black (+23 per cent). There is a 4 per cent drop in the number of White applicants.

While the number of minority ethnic applicants to teacher training programmes has increased over time, their acceptance rates remain lower than that for White applicants. There was a clear disproportionality in acceptance rates between applicants from minority ethnic backgrounds and those that identified as White (Figure 4.8). Across all years, White applicants were more likely to be accepted into training compared to Black and Other applicants. Applicants classed as Black and Other were the least likely to be accepted, with under 50 per cent accepted into ITT.

What is surprising is that 32 per cent of the 1,776 training providers with a performance profile in England had no minority ethnic applicants at all between 2014 and 2021. It is possible that many of these had fewer than three applicants, so these figures were suppressed to avoid the possibility of identifying them. A further 870 (49 per cent) had a very small number (average around five). The remaining 337 providers (19 per cent) had a total of at least 100 minority ethnic applicants over eight years. Of these, 31 (9 per cent) did not accept any of their 100 or more minority ethnic applicants.

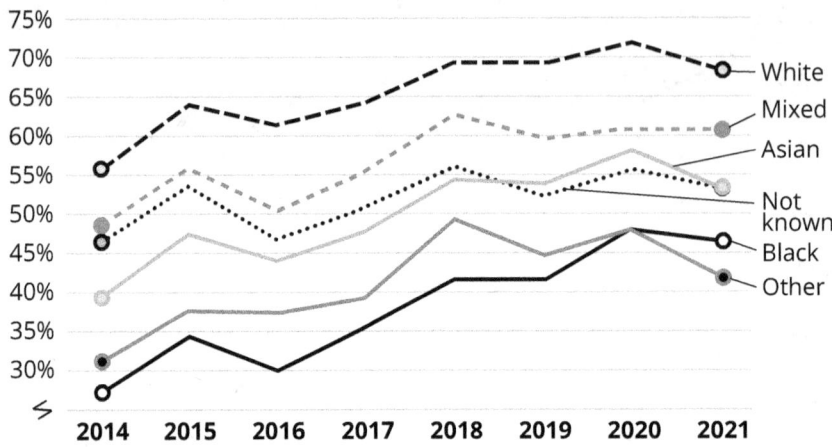

Figure 4.8 Acceptance rates to ITT (2014 to 2021)

Once accepted, minority ethnic teachers are also less likely to be awarded QTS. White teacher trainees have the highest success rate in obtaining QTS (Figure 4.9), while Pakistani, Bangladeshi, Black African and Other Black are the least likely to gain a QTS qualification. White trainees are also more likely to secure a teaching post. Minority ethnic groups, particularly those from the groups mentioned above, experience a higher dropout rate between getting QTS and securing a job in school. Even after securing a teaching role, minority ethnic teachers are less likely to stay on in the profession.

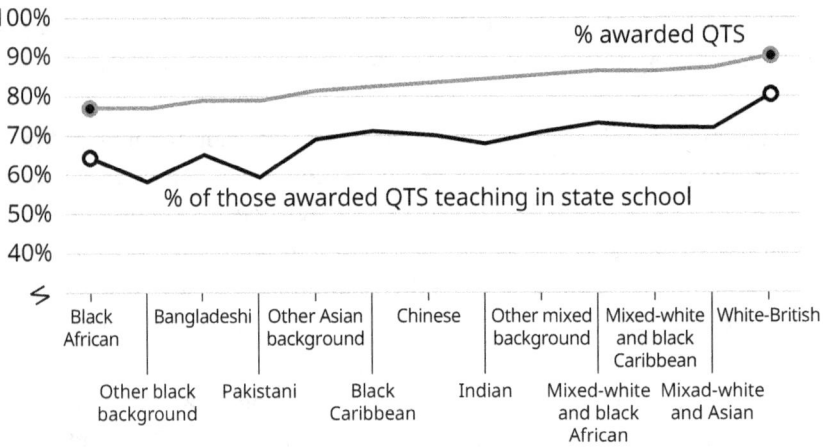

Figure 4.9 Success rates in ITT and obtaining a teaching post (2021)

These disparities in the success rates contribute significantly to the under-representation of minority ethnic teachers in the school workforce. The following section will explore potential reasons for some of these differential outcomes.

POSSIBLE EXPLANATIONS

Our review of international studies has suggested a number of possible explanations.

NEGATIVE SCHOOL EXPERIENCES

Some minority ethnic students, particularly African Caribbean, have negative school experiences, which discourage them from entering higher education and teacher training (See et al., 2011). Minority ethnic teacher trainees also reported discrimination and racism at training institutions and placement schools, including difficult mentors. This may explain the higher non-completion of training (Basit and Roberts, 2006). Although weak, some evidence suggests that minority ethnic teachers faced discrimination from staff, pupils and parents in school (Haque and Elliott, 2023).

CULTURAL AND FAMILY INFLUENCE

High-performing students are not generally interested in a career in teaching (Gorard et al., 2023b). There may be family or cultural pressures steering such students towards certain subjects and professional/vocational courses (Connor et al., 2004) and away from teaching (See et al., 2022).

ACADEMIC BARRIERS FOR ME STUDENTS

Previous studies found that some minority ethnic students, particularly Black Caribbean, Black African, Indian, Pakistani and Bangladeshi, are more likely to have lower academic attainment, reducing their chances of progressing to higher education (Gorard, 2018). They may not choose subjects that qualify for university-based teacher training. Additionally, some teacher training programmes exclude candidates with non-shortage subjects, such as sociology (Gorard et al., 2023b). Young Black Caribbean men, in particular, are less likely to follow academic pathways (Fitzgerald et al., 2000), so are less likely to qualify for teacher training courses. There is also a tendency among minority ethnic students (particularly some females) to apply to institutions geographically close to home, which may limit their choices and thus chances of success.

Studies in the US show that minority ethnic candidates were less likely to meet entry qualifications for teacher training and pass teacher certification tests (e.g. Van Overschelde and López, 2018; Motamedi et al., 2021; Williams et al., 2019). Although there is no concrete evidence from the UK to suggest that minority ethnic applicants face disadvantages in meeting entry requirements, analysis of policy reforms (See and Gorard, 2020) show that strict entry requirements to training have led to lower acceptance rates by training providers in England.

It is also possible that some ethnic groups may lack access to application processes, have lower academic qualifications, or there are cultural differences in what a good teacher looks like, which may explain why they are less successful in gaining entry to teaching. Without more information about applicants' prior attainment and other characteristics, it is hard to make any definitive conclusions, but it is clear that there is a problem in the initial supply of teachers.

STRUCTURAL AND SYSTEMIC BARRIERS

Lack of progression opportunities is another reason for the low retention of minority ethnic teachers. Previous research (e.g. Basit and Roberts, 2006; McNamara et al., 2009) has identified structural and systemic obstacles to career progression for some minority ethnic groups. These included racism and racial profiling of minority ethnic teachers' capabilities. It is important to note that these studies lack counterfactual comparison, and rely primarily on anecdotal accounts by teachers. Limited career progression may also be a retention issue for White British teacher retention, but there is no evidence that this challenge disproportionately affects minority ethnic teachers. Some studies also suggest that Black and minority ethnic teachers were more likely to have their requests for CPD denied compared to their White colleagues (Lyonette et al., 2016) or were less often encouraged to seek promotions (Harris et al., 2003). The significant under-representation of minority ethnic school leaders in England further suggests that such structural barriers exist.

IMPLICIT BIAS

Several studies have shown that minority ethnic teachers were more likely to be hired by principals of the same ethnicity (See et al., 2024), suggesting an element of implicit or unconscious bias in the wider recruitment process. This bias may act as a barrier to teachers of minority ethnicity being employed in schools. This may be, of course, just a reflection of the local and student demographic population of the school. Experimental evidence from the US (Shand and Batts, 2023) shows that anti-bias and equality, diversity and inclusion (EDI) training in two states have led to an increase in the proportion of minority ethnic teachers compared to other similar states.

WHAT CAN BE DONE?

In the short term:

- *provide tailored support to prospective minority ethnic teachers*: encourage minority ethnic students to pursue relevant degree subjects, and provide assistance with application to teacher training programmes;
- *inclusive recruitment practices*: schools could adopt blind recruitment processes and diverse hiring panels to minimise implicit bias;

- *address implicit or unconscious bias in hiring practices*: providing anti-bias and anti-racism training for school leaders and hiring committees, as in the Shands and Batts' (2023) study, can increase recruitment of minority teachers;
- *policy interventions*: government and educational institutions could introduce policies to address discrimination and structural barriers in hiring and career progression;
- *provide professional development opportunities and mentoring/induction*: this ensures minority teachers have access to career development programmes, mentorship and leadership training to overcome barriers to promotion. Some studies have also suggested that where new teachers were paired with a mentor of the same race/ethnicity, they stayed at a higher rate than those with a mentor of a different race/ethnicity (Caven et al., 2021).

In the longer term:

- *review ITT selection practices*: train interview and selection panels in ITT to recognise unconscious bias. The potential role of AI in decision-making processes for teacher recruitment to enhance diversity and equity could be considered (Klassen et al., 2023). Using AI in screening and selecting teachers for admissions to training and recruitment to complement human selections might help to address implicit bias;
- *increase diversity of school leadership*: international evidence suggests that principal-teacher race/ethnicity congruence can influence minority ethnic teachers' entry into teaching and employment. Therefore, in the long run, increasing the representation of minority ethnic groups in leadership may help reduce biases in hiring and promotion decisions;
- *encourage ethnic diversity in schools*: a diverse student population can make schools more appealing for minority ethnic teachers, which also supports retention of minority ethnic teachers;
- *improving school working conditions*: in general, improving the working conditions of schools and teaching can improve retention of all teachers, including minority ethnic teachers.

ACKNOWLEDGEMENTS

The work described here was funded by the ESRC – project number ES/X00208X/1.

FURTHER LEARNING

- Gorard S., Chen W., Tan Y. et al. (2023a) *The Disproportionality of Ethnic Minority Teachers in England: Trends, Patterns, and Problems*. London: Routledge Open Research.

  This paper highlights how minority ethnic applicants face barriers at multiple stages: acceptance into teacher training, achieving QTS and securing teaching positions. It provides insights into discrimination and disproportionality in the education sector based on analysis of multiple datasets. It suggests actionable steps, such as better teacher preparation for diverse classrooms and increased scrutiny of acceptance rates by regulatory bodies.

- See B.H., Gorard S., Gao Y. et al. (2024) Factors related to the recruitment and retention of ethnic minority teachers: what are the barriers and facilitators? *Review of Education* 12(3): e70005.

This paper highlights the barriers that minority ethnic prospective teachers face and offers evidence-based solutions to improve diversity in the teaching workforce. It identifies structural barriers to teaching, such as the entry qualifications and assessment criteria, which may unintentionally exclude minority ethnic applicants. While there is no strong evidence that alternative certification increases minority ethnic teacher recruitment, there are supportive features that could help. Addressing implicit bias, closing disparities in entry requirements, having more minority ethnic school leaders and using AI in screening and selecting teachers (to mitigate against bias in hiring and selection of teachers) are suggested actions to take to increase the supply of minority ethnic teachers.

- Gorard S., Gao Y., See B.H. et al. (2025) What helps to attract minority ethnic teachers in England? Results from a national survey. *Review of Education Studies* 5(1):50–75.

This paper identifies stress as the most important predictor of teachers wanting to leave the profession, making this an urgent issue to be addressed. Another important factor in keeping minority ethnic teachers is supportive school leaders. While racism and individual teacher ethnicity are less important factors in predicting teacher attrition, the overall ethnic diversity of school leaders, staff and students is an important influencing factor. Reducing ethnic segregation in schools would create a fairer system and support minority ethnic teacher retention.

REFERENCES

Bailes, L. and Guthery, S. (2020) Held down and held back: systematically delayed principal promotions by race and gender. *AERA Open*, 6(2), 2332858420929298.

Bartanen, B. and Grissom, J. (2019) School principal race and the hiring and retention of racially diverse teachers (EdWorking Paper No. 19, 59). Annenberg Institute at Brown University.

Basit, T. and Roberts, L (2006) *Tackling Racism in School Placements: Final Report to Multiverse*. London: Multiverse.

Blom, E., Lindsay, C. and Tilsley, A. (2017) *Diversifying the Classroom: Examining the Teacher Pipeline*. Washington, DC: Urban Institute.

Carver-Thomas, D. (2018) *Diversifying the Teaching Profession: How to Recruit and Retain Teachers of Color*. Palo Alto, CA: Learning Policy Institute.

Caven, M., Durodoye, R., Zhang, X. and Bock, G. (2021) Variation in mentoring practices and retention across new teacher demographic characteristics under a large urban district's new teacher mentoring program. REL 2021-100. National Center for Education Evaluation and Regional Assistance, Institute of Education Sciences.

Connor, H., Tyers, C., Modood, T. and Hillage, J. (2004) *Why the Difference? A Closer Look at Higher Education Minority Ethnic Students and Graduates*. Nottingham: DfES. Research Report 552

Dee, T. (2005) A teacher like me: does race, ethnicity, or gender matter? *American Economic Review*, 95(2), 158–65.

Demie, F. and See, B.H. (2023) Ethnic disproportionality in the school teaching workforce in England. *Equity in Education and Society*, 2(1), 3–27.

Fitzgerald, R., Finch, S. and Nove, A. (2000) *Black Caribbean Young Men's Experiences of Education and Employment*. Nottingham: DfES. Research Report 186.

Gershenson, S., Hart, C., Hyman, J., Lindsay, C., and Papageorge, N. (2022) The long-run impacts of same-race teachers. *American Economic Journal: Economic Policy*, 14(4), 300–42.

Gershenson, S., Holt, S. and Papageorge, N. (2016) Who believes in me? The effect of student–teacher demographic match on teacher expectations. *Economics of Education Review*, 52, 209–24.

Goff, P., Rodriguez-Escutia, Y. and Yang, M. (2018) Through the labor market looking glass: an inquiry into principal-teacher race congruence (WCER Working Paper No. 2018-13). Wisconsin Center for Education Research.

Gorard, S. (2018) *Education Policy*. Bristol: Policy Press

Gorard, S. and Smith, E. (2010) *Equity in Education: An International Comparison of Pupil Perspectives*. London: Palgrave

Gorard, S., Chen, W., Tan, Y., See, B.H., Gazmuri, C., Tereshchenko, A., Demie, F. and Siddiqui, N. (2023a) *The Disproportionality of Ethnic Minority Teachers in England: Trends, Patterns, and Problems*. London: Routledge Open Research.

Gorard, S., Gao, Y., See, B.H., Tereshchenko, A., Siddiqui, N. and Demie, F. (2025) What helps to attract minority ethnic teachers in England? Results from a national survey. *Review of Education Studies*, 5(1), 50–75.

Gorard, S., Ventista, O., Morris, R. and See, B.H. (2023b) Who wants to be a teacher? Findings from a survey of undergraduates in England. *Educational Studies*, 49(6), 914–36.

gov.uk (2018) *Diversity of the Teaching Workforce*. DfE. Available at: https://www.gov.uk/government/publications/diversity-of-the-teaching-workforce-statement-of-intent (accessed: 25 April 2025).

gov.uk (2021a) *Initial Teacher Training Performance Profiles*. Available at: https://explore-education-statistics.service.gov.uk/find-statistics/initial-teacher-training-performance-profiles (accessed: 25 April 2025).

gov.uk (2021b) *School Teacher Workforce*. Available at: www.ethnicity-facts-figures.service.gov.uk/workforce-and-business/workforce-diversity/school-teacher-workforce/latest#:~:text=Percentage%20and%20number%20of%20school%20teachers%20by%20ethnicity,%20%207%2C200%20%2019%20more%20rows%20 (accessed: 25 April 2025).

Grissom, J. and Redding, C. (2016) Discretion and disproportionality: explaining the under-representation of high-achieving students of color in gifted programs. *AERA Open*, 2(1), https://doi.org/10.1177/2332858415622175

Grissom, J., Kern, E. and Rodriguez, L. (2017) *Teacher and Principal Diversity and the Representation of Students of Color in Gifted Programs: Evidence from National Data*. Chicago: University of Chicago Press.

Grissom, J., Nicholson-Crotty, J. and Nicholson-Crotty, S. (2009) Race, region, and representative bureaucracy. *Public Administration Review*, 69, 911–19.

Haque, Z. and Elliott, S. (2023) *Barriers: Visible and Invisible Barriers. The Impact of Racism on BME Teachers*. London: Runnymede Trust.

Harris, A., Mujis, D., Crawford, M. (2003) *Deputy and Assistant Head: Building Leadership Potential*. Nottingham: National College for the Leadership of Schools and Children's Services.

Ingersoll, R., May, H. and Collins, G. (2017) *Minority Teacher Recruitment, Employment, and Retention: 1987 to 2013*. Londobn: Learning Policy Institute.

Ingersoll, R., May, H. and Collins, G. (2019) Recruitment, employment, retention and the minority teacher shortage. *Education Policy Analysis Archives*, 27, 37.

Klassen, R., Wang, H. and Rushby, J. (2023) Can an online scenario-based learning intervention influence preservice teachers' self-efficacy, career intentions, and perceived fit with the profession? *Computers and Education*, 207, 104935.

Lindsay, C. (2017) *Teachers of Color are Less Likely to be Teaching than their White Counterparts*. Washington, DC: Urban Wire.

Lindsay, C. and Hart, C. (2017) Exposure to same-race teachers and student disciplinary outcomes for Black students in North Carolina. *Educational Evaluation and Policy Analysis*, 39(3), 485–51.

Lyonette, C., Atfield, G., Barnes, S.A. and Owen, D. (2016) *Teachers' Pay and Equality: Online Survey and Qualitative Study. Longitudinal Research into the Impact of Changes to Teachers' Pay on Equality in Schools in England*. Warwick: Warwick Institute for Employment Research.

McNamara, O., Howson, J. Gunter, H. and Fryers, A. (2009) *Supporting the Leadership Aspirations and Careers of Black and Minority Ethnic Teachers*. Birmingham: NASUWT.

Motamedi, J., Yoon, S. and Hanson, H. (2021) *Pathways to teaching: teacher diversity, testing, certification, and employment in Washington State (REL 2021-094)*. Regional Educational Laboratory Northwest.

Scottish Government (2021) *Teaching in a Diverse Scotland*. Available at: www.gov.scot/publications/teaching-diverse-scotland-increasing-retaining-minority-ethnic-teachers-3-years/ (accessed: 25 April 2025).

See, B.H. and Gorard, S. (2020) Why don't we have enough teachers? A reconsideration of the available evidence. *Research Papers in Education*, 35(4), 416–42.

See, B.H., Gorard, S., Gao, Y., Hitt, L., Siddiqui, N., Demie, F., Tereshchenko, A. and El Soufi, N. (2024) Factors related to the recruitment and retention of ethnic minority teachers: what are the barriers and facilitators? *Review of Education*, 12(3), e70005.

See, B.H., Munthe, E., Ross, S., Hitt, L., and El Soufi, N. (2022) Who becomes a teacher and why? *Review of Education*, 10(3), 1–40.

See, B.H., Torgerson, C., Gorard, S., Ainsworth, H., Low, G. and Wright, K. (2011) Factors that promote high post-16 participation of some minority ethnic groups in England: a systematic review of the UK-based literature. *Research in Post-Compulsory Education*, 16(1), 85–100.

Shand, R. and Batts, J. (2023) Toward more inclusive professional learning communities. *Journal of Education Human Resources*, 41(1), 110–41.

Shiner, M. and Modood, T. (2002) Help or hindrance? Higher education and the route to ethnic equality. *British Journal of Sociology of Education*, 23(2), 209–32.

Stiefel, L., Syeda, S., Cimpian, J. and O'Hagan, K. (2022) The role of school context in explaining racial disproportionality in special education. EdWorkingPaper: 22–661,

US Department of Education (2016) *The State of Racial Diversity in the Educator Workforce, Office of Planning, Evaluation and Policy Development*. Policy and Program Studies Service, Washington, DC.

Van Overschelde, J. and López, M. (2018) Raising the bar or locking the door? The effects of increasing GPA admission requirements on teacher preparation. *Equity and Excellence in Education*, 51(3–4), 223–41.

Welsh Government (2023) *Launch of Incentive to a More Diverse Teaching Workforce*. Available at: https://businesswales.gov.wales/news-and-blog/launch-incentive-attract-a-more-diverse-teaching-workforce (accessed: 25 April 2025).

Williams, J., Hart, L. and Algozzine, B. (2019) Perception vs reality: EdTPA perceptions and performance for teacher candidates of color and White candidates. *Teaching and Teacher Education*, 83, 120–33.

Wright, A. (2015) Teachers' perceptions of students' disruptive behavior. Association for Education Finance and Policy Annual Conference. Available at: www.researchgate.net/publication/342339365_Teachers%27_Perceptions_of_Students%27_Disruptive_Behavior_The_Effect_of_Racial_Congruence_and_Consequences_for_School_Suspension (accessed 24 February 2025).

PART 2
INCLUSIVE LEADERSHIP
STRATEGIES FOR SUPPORTING DIVERSE STAFF TEAMS

5

INCLUSIVE LEADERSHIP

ADDRESSING SYSTEMIC BARRIERS TO SUPPORT TEACHERS FROM MINORITY ETHNIC BACKGROUNDS

ANGELA BROWNE AND SUFIAN SADIQ

INTRODUCTION

The UK teaching workforce exhibits significant racial inequality, characterised by the under-representation of teachers from minority ethnic backgrounds across all career stages, particularly in leadership roles. This disparity persists despite a growing proportion of ethnically diverse students in UK schools. As a school leader, you play a pivotal role in fostering a more inclusive and equitable school culture – one where all teachers are valued and have access to meaningful career progression.

Understanding the structural challenges that limit representation is the first step in enacting meaningful change. This chapter explores the systemic barriers that contribute to the under-representation of minority ethnic teachers in leadership and recommends adopting a human-centred approach to leadership as the first step towards addressing these obstacles. By the end of this chapter, you will have a deeper understanding of the systemic barriers that impact teachers from minority ethnic backgrounds, the importance of inclusive leadership in addressing these inequities and practical strategies to create supportive and equitable school environments.

UNDER-REPRESENTATION IN THE TEACHING WORKFORCE

The issue of under-representation of minority ethnic teachers in the UK's education system is not uniform across the nation. While teachers from White ethnic backgrounds are spread across different regions, there is a significant variation in the geographic distribution of educators from minority ethnic backgrounds. Cities with more diverse populations such as London, Birmingham, Manchester, Leicester, Bradford and Luton tend to have a higher proportion of minority ethnic teachers compared to other regions (Tereshchenko et al., 2020). In 2020/1, London accounted for a disproportionately high percentage of teachers from Asian (39 per cent), Black (62 per cent), Mixed (37 per cent) and Other (53 per cent) ethnic backgrounds compared to their White counterparts (11 per cent) (Worth et al., 2022). This concentration, while providing some visibility within these diverse urban areas, masks the acute under-representation in more geographically dispersed areas. A majority of schools in England (60 per cent) have no teachers from minority ethnic backgrounds, and this is particularly pronounced outside diverse urban areas (Worth et al., 2022).

When these major urban hubs are factored out, the picture of minority ethnic teacher representation becomes considerably bleaker. Certain regions, such as the South West and specific pockets like the North East coastal towns, exhibit particularly low levels of representation. This lack of visibility and representation can have significant implications for the school community, contributing to a less inclusive culture with a paucity of experiences, perspectives and understanding that can affect all staff and pupils. A diverse teaching workforce can promote social cohesion, support pupils' cultural understanding and foster an environment in which teachers of all ethnicities can progress and thrive.

TEACHER TRAINING AND ACCEPTANCE

Why is there a lack of ethnic diversity in the teaching workforce? Addressing this question involves looking at the very beginning of the journey towards becoming a teacher. While minority ethnic individuals are frequently over-represented among applicants to initial teacher training (ITT) programmes, they are significantly less likely to receive and accept an offer compared to their White peers. This strongly suggests the presence of institutional racism embedded within application and assessment processes. While London has a smaller overall gap in ITT acceptance rates compared to other regions, likely due to its diverse population, significant disparities persist nationally (Worth et al., 2022). ITT data reveals 'striking disproportionality in acceptance rates, with Black applicants least likely to be accepted' (Demie et al., 2023). Research by the NFER found that all ethnic groups except White are under-represented at all career stages of the teaching profession, except for ITT (Worth et al., 2022). The report's data shows that in 2019/20, people from White ethnic backgrounds were under-represented among postgraduate ITT applicants, but over-represented from ITT enrolment onwards. Conversely, successful applicants from Black backgrounds were under-represented by one percentage point at the stage of enrolment onto postgraduate ITT and remained under-represented throughout all other stages of the profession. This over-representation at the application stage, followed by under-representation from enrolment onwards, points to systemic issues within ITT selection processes.

The lower ITT acceptance rates for teachers from minority ethnic backgrounds, despite their higher application numbers, likely stems from racial bias (conscious and unconscious) or inequity in applications and assessment processes that means these applicants are unfairly disadvantaged. Negative experiences during ITT also contribute to fewer trainee teachers of colour achieving qualified teacher status (QTS). The journeys of Black and Asian student teachers through ITT can be 'fraught with suffering, often resulting from multitudes of (racial) microaggressions' (Demie et al, 2023; Warner, 2022). These student teachers report feeling less equipped and supported by their ITT tutors and school mentors and experience a critical absence of discussion on race issues, leading to self-censoring and marginalisation. Early career teachers (ECTs) interviewed for a Mission 44-funded project aimed at increasing the proportion of ethnically diverse teachers entering the teaching profession with the Chartered College of Teaching, Chiltern Learning Trust and Being Luminary, recounted multiple experiences of racism, often from other staff. The anxiety about reporting racism, fearing being labelled as an 'angry Black/Brown person', further compounds these negative experiences. These challenges within ITT not only impact QTS attainment, but also contribute to disillusionment with the profession early on.

INSTITUTIONAL RACISM IN THE TEACHING PROFESSION

Once qualified and working as teachers, people from minority ethnic backgrounds often continue to encounter the effects of institutional racism. Overt and covert racial discrimination impacts daily experiences, hindering professional growth and wellbeing, and ultimately contributing to lower retention rates. In contrast to the medical profession, for example, where objective exams provide a more meritocratic pathway, teaching relies heavily on subjective assessments by mentors who may lack adequate training or awareness of their own biases. This subjectivity can unfairly disadvantage minority ethnic trainees and teachers, as well as individuals with other protected characteristics.

Minority ethnic teachers frequently face racist stereotyping. A senior leader interviewed by Education Support recounted being directed to the kitchen instead of the main hall on their first day as a newly qualified Black teacher (Education Support, 2023). A survey by the teachers' union the NASUWT in 2016 found that 31 per cent of Black and minority ethnic teachers had experienced discrimination in their workplace. Beyond individual acts, schools can operate as 'White spaces' – social environments where Whiteness is the norm, and people of colour are viewed as outsiders (Education and Childhood Research Group, 2023). This isolation not only significantly affects the wellbeing of minority ethnic teachers and their motivation to stay in the profession, it also limits career trajectories in a way that is impossible to challenge if a school does not acknowledge the existence of institutional racism and how racial bias operates.

Racism can be nuanced and expressed in different ways, occurring even when school leaders might believe that they have created an open and welcoming environment. A prevalent example of this is intellectual racism, in which, despite increasing diversity in institutions, minority ethnic teachers are encouraged into pastoral roles rather than being recognised for their expertise and interests in teaching and learning. Assumptions are made that Black and Asian teachers will excel in areas such as behaviour management, leading to them being 'funnelled' into these areas against their preferences. In contrast, White British graduates might be more readily directed towards teaching and learning leadership roles based on assumptions of their intellect. This pigeonholing limits opportunities for minority ethnic teachers to progress in curriculum leadership, pedagogy and assessment.

Lack of representative leadership in schools, particularly in diverse urban settings, is another significant challenge. Senior leadership teams that do not reflect the diversity of the student intake and staff at more junior levels could indicate an organisational culture that may be colour-blind and hostile to work in. The racial literacy of senior leadership teams, leading to clear progression pathways, is crucial to supporting and retaining teachers from minority ethnic backgrounds. As one teacher articulated in research by the Institute of Education (IOE, UCL), senior leaders cannot effectively address race-related complaints without understanding the nuances of contemporary racism (Tereshchenko et al., 2020).

Stalled opportunities for career progression represent a critical barrier for experienced minority ethnic teachers. Many report feeling unfairly passed over for senior posts, encountering a *glass ceiling* that limits their advancement beyond middle leadership roles. The lack of visible progression pathways can lead to disillusionment and the pursuit of roles outside the state school sector. The NFER found that people from White ethnic backgrounds are more likely than those from other ethnic backgrounds to progress from each stage of the teaching profession to the next, apart from progression to middle leadership. While teachers from Black backgrounds are more likely to be promoted to middle leadership than their White counterparts before accounting for other characteristics, this advantage disappears and reverses after considering factors like the regions and types of schools they tend to work in. For example, teachers from minority ethnic backgrounds are more likely to work in specific regions (like London) and in secondary schools, where promotion rates to middle leadership are generally higher for all ethnic groups. Once these differences in characteristics are statistically controlled for, the picture changes.

ROLE MODELS AND INTELLECTUAL RACISM

It is vital for leaders to reflect critically on why there might be a lack of teachers from minority ethnic backgrounds applying to work in their schools, and why these teachers might leave or not progress once employed. Among networks of teachers from minority ethnic groups, the perception of a school and their organisational culture matters. If a teacher experiences racial bias they may, as with other negative experiences, share this with their peers, which will discourage applications and compound the issue of under-representation in certain schools and areas.

School leaders are, of course, very unlikely to see their school culture as marginalising – environments that are exclusionary can develop even with well-intentioned efforts. For example, as mentioned briefly earlier, the concept of minority ethnic teachers serving as *role models* is frequently invoked as a reason to diversify the teaching profession, often with the aim of highlighting the positive impact they can have on students, particularly those from similar ethnic backgrounds. While some minority ethnic teachers may be motivated to teach in diverse schools, feeling a sense of responsibility to represent and support students from similar backgrounds – and research suggests that teachers of colour can improve the academic outcomes and reduce school exclusions of minority ethnic pupils – solely framing minority ethnic teachers as role models is severely limiting. Teachers of all ethnicities have a range of motivations for getting into teaching, including a love of their subject, enjoying working with young people and wanting to make a difference. Within Islam, teaching is seen as a noble and virtuous profession, and this respect for teaching is shared among many communities and cultures – teaching is one of the oldest professions, and if people with protected characteristics are not entering or progressing it is necessary to look inward at why they are being kept out and the barriers they are facing.

The assumption that Black and Asian teachers are naturally suited for behaviour management roles, while White teachers are steered towards teaching and learning leadership, exemplifies one damaging form of racial bias. This can stem from unconscious biases that associate certain ethnicities with specific skill sets or areas of expertise (or lack thereof). This stereotyping not only limits the professional growth and career progression of minority ethnic teachers, but also deprives the wider school community of their teaching abilities and perspectives across all areas of education. It reinforces a subtle hierarchy where the intellectual contributions of minority ethnic educators are devalued or narrowly defined. Addressing this requires a conscious effort to move beyond simplistic role model narratives and recognise the capabilities and aspirations of all teachers.

SYSTEMIC BARRIERS AND TEACHER RETENTION

The confluence of geographic disparities, institutional biases in recruitment and progression, experiences of discrimination and the limiting framing of role models contribute to systemic barriers that impact the retention of minority ethnic teachers. The job satisfaction and retention of minority ethnic teachers are also affected by the intersection of race and racism with other aspects of identity, such as gender and class, with Black teachers particularly disadvantaged. The education system has not developed to support either ethnic or intersectional diversity and requires systemic change rather than isolated initiatives. The persistent gap between the proportion of minority ethnic students and teachers over time suggests a lack of progress in race equality within the education system (Tereshchenko et al., 2020).

Interestingly, workload is not the primary concern for minority ethnic teachers regarding retention, unlike their White British colleagues (Tereshchenko et al., 2020). Instead, dealing with the consequences of racial discrimination and inequalities is in itself a type of hidden workload, contributing to burnout and turnover. The constant need to navigate microaggressions, challenge stereotypes and advocate for equitable treatment takes a significant emotional and psychological toll. Anxiety about reporting racism further exacerbates this hidden workload – if a school does not have policies in place to identify and address racism, there is no way for teachers to report their experience or for the school to change their organisational culture.

The absence of strong support networks and mentors who understand the specific cultural contexts and challenges faced by minority ethnic teachers also contributes to retention issues. Feeling isolated in predominantly White environments can be a major factor in the decision to leave. Schools with a higher proportion of minority ethnic staff, where supportive networks can develop, tend to have better retention rates for these teachers. Establishing mentoring and support networks is important for improving the experiences and retention of minority ethnic educators. Teachers who were part of larger networks (multi-academy trust (MAT)-wide, regional and national groups) interviewed for a project aimed at increasing the proportion of ethnically diverse teachers entering the teaching profession reported that it was useful to have people to turn to when racist incidents occurred and people who generally 'get it'. Establishing buddy schemes – structured support systems that pair minority ethnic teachers with experienced colleagues – can also support inclusion and provide a safe space for discussion and challenge. Similarly, developing networking opportunities can support teachers with navigating the school environment.

CULTURAL CAPITAL AND HUMAN-CENTRED LEADERSHIP

Addressing systemic issues requires a fundamental shift in school culture and leadership approaches. Developing cultural capital among White teachers is a productive step towards this. Some White teachers may have limited personal interaction with individuals from certain minority ethnic communities and may lack understanding of their lived experiences. Building cultural capital involves fostering awareness, understanding and empathy towards a range of cultural backgrounds and perspectives. This also includes recognising one's own privilege.

Adopting human-centred leadership supports the development of an inclusive school culture. This approach prioritises building genuine relationships, actively listening to concerns and valuing the experiences and perspectives of all staff. For example, conducting exit interviews specifically targeted at understanding the experiences of departing minority ethnic teachers can provide valuable insights into systemic issues and inform necessary changes. At the beginning of a teacher's journey, being proactive about making someone feel welcome, such as ensuring names are pronounced correctly and asking about and remembering the names of children and family members, can go a long way in making trainees feel a sense of belonging. Careful consideration of school placement for trainees, avoiding situations where they are the only person of colour, is also crucial.

Leaders need to be equipped to make equitable decisions, and progress towards equalising opportunities for progression should be actively monitored. This requires a commitment to fair treatment, addressing racism proactively through anti-racist training for mentors and leaders and developing transparent systems for reporting racist incidents. Challenging stereotypes, removing tokenism and actively promoting progression pathways for teachers of colour are essential leadership responsibilities. The NFER recommends that school leaders in diverse schools should be asked by stakeholders to demonstrate the experience, training and skills that allow them to develop equitable learning environments that support minority ethnic teachers.

ENSHRINING ANTI-RACIST PRACTICES

To achieve meaningful and sustainable change, anti-racist principles must be embedded within the fabric of school policies and practices. Of course, this goes beyond surface-level statements of commitment to equality and requires a deep and ongoing process of review, revision and implementation of policies that actively challenge and dismantle racial biases. This involves developing policies to ensure that everyone has the same starting point and that safeguards are in place to bring the experience of minority ethnic teachers up to the average experience of everyone in the institution.

Training for all staff and leadership teams on anti-racism and whole-school diversity and inclusion initiatives are essential in the longer term. The National Education Union's Anti-Racist Charter (available at https://neu.org.uk) and the London Borough of Lambeth's anti-racist framework are helpful examples of practical tools for tackling racism in schools. However, the first step is for leaders to reflect critically on their current knowledge and practices. Work in equity, diversity and inclusion can end up becoming a tick-box exercise if there is a lack of understanding of institutional racism and racial bias. Building understanding and cultural capital involves genuinely listening and seeking out the views of teachers with protected characteristics to understand how the intersection of race and other aspects of identity impact a teacher's experience of working and progressing in your school. This should be part of a broader organisational culture in which senior leadership teams are empowered to identify and address behaviour and practices that limit opportunities for or negatively affect minority ethnic teachers or pupils.

Implementing anti-racist practices also involves a commitment to transparency and accountability. Schools need to develop clear and trusted systems for reporting racism, ensuring that individuals feel safe and supported in raising concerns without fear of reprisal. Progress towards greater representation and equitable outcomes should be regularly monitored and evaluated. This requires the collection and analysis of data on recruitment, retention, progression and experiences of racism, broken down by ethnicity, to identify areas where disparities persist and to measure the impact of implemented policies.

CONCLUSION

The significant and persistent under-representation and inequality faced by minority ethnic teachers within the UK education system points to a systemic issue. The challenges begin at the point of entry into the profession, with discriminatory practices within ITT, and continue throughout their careers in the form of discrimination, limited progression opportunities and the burden of navigating racial biases.

Addressing these entrenched challenges requires a multifaceted and sustained effort grounded in a commitment to anti-racist principles – a genuine understanding of the principles must come before trying to initiate change in practice in order for it to be sustainable and meaningful in the long term.

School leaders have a crucial role to play in fostering inclusive recruitment practices, developing cultural capital among staff, adopting human-centred leadership approaches and developing inclusive policies that are consistently implemented. Monitoring career progression opportunities for all staff, investigating claims of racism and actively working to dismantle systemic barriers, such as by recognising and moving beyond limiting stereotypes, are important steps. Working towards the creation of a truly equitable and inclusive teaching profession will not only benefit minority ethnic teachers, but will also enrich the educational experiences and outcomes of all students.

FURTHER LEARNING

- Wilkins, C. and Lall, R. (2011) You've got to be tough and I'm trying: Black and minority ethnic student teachers' experiences of initial teacher education. *Race Ethnicity and Education*, 14(3), 365–86.

This article documents the social isolation, stereotypical attitudes from White peers and instances of overt racism, particularly during school placements, that Black and minority ethnic student teachers face. It argues that fostering an inclusive and supportive environment is crucial to address these challenges and to prevent marginalisation.

- Tereshchenko, A., Kaur, B., Cara, O., Wiggins, A. and Pillinger, C. (2024). Racial microaggressions on the initial teacher education programmes: implications for minority ethnic teacher retention. *Teachers and Teaching*. Advance online publication, 1–19. Available at: https://doi.org/10.1080/13540602.2024.2397583 (accessed 28 April 2025).

This study highlights how racial microaggressions in initial teacher education (ITE) programmes, especially during school placements, negatively impact minority ethnic student teachers. It emphasises the need for more inclusive and supportive environments to improve teacher retention.

REFERENCES

Demie, F., Maude, K. and Race, R. (2023) Ethnic Inequality in the Teaching Workforce in Schools: *Why It Matters. British Educational Research Association.* Available at: www.bera.ac.uk/blog/ethnic-inequality-in-the-teaching-workforce-in-schools-why-it-matters. (accessed 14 March 2024).

Education and Childhood Research Group (2023) *More Ethnic Minority Teachers are needed in UK Schools – But Teaching can Affect Their Mental Health and Wellbeing.* Available at; https://blogs.uwe.ac.uk/education/more-ethnic-minority-teachers-are-needed-in-uk-schools-but-teaching-can-affect-their-mental-health-and-wellbeing/ (accessed: 14 March 2024).

Education Support (2023) *Mental Health and Wellbeing of Ethnic Minority Teachers.* Available at: www.educationsupport.org.uk/media/painjg2z/mental-health-and-wellbeing-of-ethnic-minority-teachers.pdf (accessed: 14 March 2024).

NASUWT (2016) *Visible Minorities, Invisible Teachers: BME Teachers in the Education System in England.* Available at: www.nasuwt.org.uk/static/uploaded/6576a736-87d3-4a21-837fd1a1ea4aa2c5.pdf (accessed: 14 March 2024).

Tereshchenko, A., Mills, M. and Bradbury, A. (2020) *Making Progress? Employment and Retention of BAME Teachers in England.* London: UCL Institute of Education. Available at: https://discovery.ucl.ac.uk/id/eprint/10117331/ (accessed: 14 March 2024).

Warner, D. (2022) Black and minority ethnic student teachers' stories as empirical documents of hidden oppressions: using the personal to turn towards the structural. *British Educational Research Journal, 48(6),* 1145–60. doi.org/10.1002/berj.3819 (accessed: 14 March 2024).

Worth, J., McLean, D. and Sharp, C. (2022) *Racial Equality in the Teacher Workforce.* National Foundation for Educational Research. Available at: www.nfer.ac.uk/publications/racial-equality-in-the-teacher-workforce/ (accessed: 14 March 2024).

6
RECRUITING AND SUPPORTING NEURODIVERGENT TEACHERS BY DEVELOPING AN INCLUSIVE WORK ENVIRONMENT

CLAIRE O'NEILL

INTRODUCTION

This chapter explores what we know about neurodivergent teachers and how school leaders can best recruit, support and retain this minority group. Centring around an organising model called the LEARNING Framework (Figure 6.1), the chapter supports school leaders to:

- deepen their understanding of inclusion from a neurodiversity-informed perspective;
- explore key factors influencing the recruiting, supporting and retaining of neurodivergent teaching staff;

- use a framework containing practical suggestions to support those new to the profession while enabling all staff members to progress;
- access tools to address some of the barriers that neurodivergent teachers might face including early career stages and progressing into leadership positions.

NEURODIVERGENT TEACHERS

The field of knowledge relating to neurodivergent learners and inclusion is broad and expanding (for example, see Goodall, 2020; Montero et al., 2023). In contrast, the literature relating to neurodivergent teachers, although growing, is still sparse. Examples of this literature include articles relating to teachers with dyslexia (Burns and Bell, 2011; Riddick, 2003) and teachers with ADHD (Harris, 2024). However, most studies focus on teachers with autism (for example, Baird, 2020; Lawrence, 2019; O'Neill and Kenny, 2023). The first section of this chapter gives a brief overview of the recruitment and support of neurodivergent teachers before introducing the LEARNING Framework, a model used to highlight pertinent issues for school leaders wishing to be more inclusive in their approach towards their neurodivergent colleagues.

RECRUITING NEURODIVERGENT TEACHERS

Sourcing accurate information and advice on recruiting and retaining neurodivergent teachers is a task that requires effort. More generalised neurodivergent-focused literature related to workplace and employment offers some guidance, but fails to encompass the specificity needed for the unique qualities of teaching as a profession and of schools as workplace environments. Some areas for consideration are listed here:

1. Inclusive advertising of teaching positions. Principles of universal design can help with designing an advertisement that is accessible to a broad range of candidates. This might include:
   - clearly communicated role description that takes into consideration how a neurodivergent candidate might interpret the description;
   - transparent, bullet-pointed steps guiding the candidate through the application process;
   - use of ALT text and accessibility features like contrast and adaptable font size. Text should be shared in a way that allows for text to speech software.
2. Share as much specific information about the interview as you can and consider giving interview questions or at least general topics in advance.

3. Explicitly communicate that you are willing to make equitable adjustments to the recruitment process and share details of how these adjustments can be arranged.
4. Be aware of possible bias in the selection process. For example, what is your reaction to eye contact that differs from what you typically expect or answers to questions that might demonstrate thinking about a competency in a novel way?
5. Give constructive feedback and ask for feedback from candidates.

SUPPORTING NEURODIVERGENT TEACHERS

Accurate and focused content for school leaders wishing to support and retain existing neurodivergent staff is not easy to find. However, the growing body of literature based on participatory approaches provides us with useful knowledge when it comes to retaining and supporting neurodivergent teachers and this will be explored further later on in the chapter. In the first instance, a well-developed inclusive school culture is an essential starting point when seeking to support neurodivergent teachers.

DEVELOPING AN INCLUSIVE WORK ENVIRONMENT

It is noteworthy that workplaces that have a solid record in other areas of diversity and inclusion are more likely to be environments in which neurodivergent people can thrive and flourish (Romualdez et al., 2021). In my experience as a busy school leader, scaffolding, often in the form of a framework, is essential in operationalising an impactful and successful change process. A shared framework offers commonality, simplicity and transparency – all critical factors in implementation, collaboration and school development (Kantawala, 2023). In the context of developing inclusive practice, several suitable frameworks exist including those reviewed by Kefallinou et al. (2020). However, here our specific focus is the inclusion and support of neurodivergent teachers and, that being so, the chapter uses a neurodivergent-designed framework directly informed by the experiences of teachers with autism. The LEARNING Framework is a multi-functional organising model (Figure 6.1) and provides a conceptual map for those wishing to operationalise a vision for a more inclusive workplace into goals and actions.

THE LEARNING FRAMEWORK

As the focus shifts from the general to granulated, this second section offers practical advice for leaders; this content is presented under the components of the LEARNING Framework (Figure 6.1). In addition, the framework is supported by findings from key literature and direct quotes from teachers with autism who have shared their experiences of schools as workplaces (O'Neill and Kenny, 2023). By engaging with this framework-based section of the chapter, school leaders will have a scaffold to create a more neurodiversity-inclusive school environment.

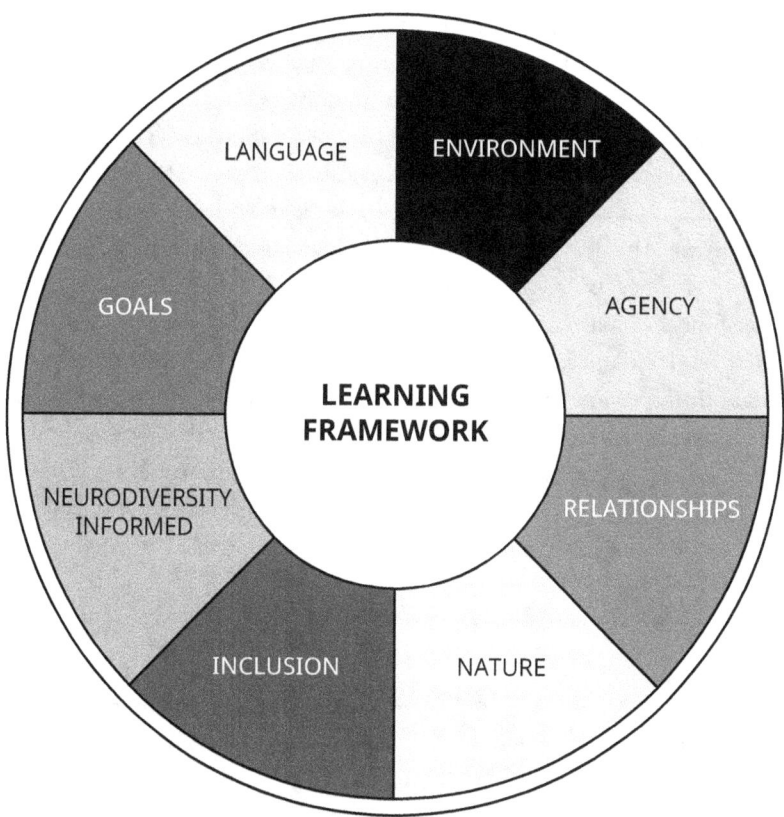

Figure 6.1 The LEARNING Framework (O'Neill, 2024)

PRACTICAL ADVICE FOR SCHOOL LEADERS: USING THE LEARNING FRAMEWORK

This section gives practical suggestions of key areas of focus to better support neurodivergent teachers.

Language

I think it's seen more as almost a disease. I don't think people really understand … people were saying 'Oh she's autistic' in a really negative way.

Bridget

The language we choose to use as school leaders and educators is a critical factor in creating a safe, inclusive and respectful workplace environment for all members of the school community.

The connection between language and neurodivergent teachers is a key consideration in creating authentically inclusive experiences. For example, medicalised and pathologising language commonly associated with autism and other neurominorities is a clear barrier to inclusion (Bury et al., 2023). The neurodiversity paradigm offers a solid rationale for eschewing medicalised language and offers alternative and affirmative options (Walker, 2021). As more research with and by neurodivergent individuals enters the field, the lexicon used to convey neurodivergent experience also grows. This is a push back to pathologising and stigmatising language considered an epistemic violence by some researchers (Botha, 2021; Catala et al., 2021), a form of microaggression found in learning environments and the workplace which can contribute to minority stress. School leaders can support neurodivergent teachers by critically examining the language used both informally and more formally at school level. Moreover, neurodivergent teachers report that experiences of non-inclusive language are experienced across all levels of education systems. On a practical level, this tasks school leaders not only to be aware of language at a school level, but also to advocate for inclusive language with outside agencies and professionals and to be critically aware of the language used in policy documents and at professional training sessions.

Environment

> *Corridors for me are a nightmare. There's a bombardment of the senses all the time. I'm in an internal panic. I can't cope on that level because I'm here (hand to top of head) with sensory stuff, there's no room left.*
>
> Ciara

The relationship between neurodivergent teachers and the school environment provides rich insights into how the physical environment can nurture or thwart inclusion. A clear finding from the available research is that aspects of the indoor environment are challenging for neurodivergent teachers and many of the challenges are related to the sensory environment. In contrast, however, other aspects of the school environment, including classrooms, are often experienced as havens of inclusivity. This aligns with Nind et al., who describe how school environments can foster a sense of belonging or exclusion (2022).

Agency

Issues of agency, which include honouring neurodivergent expertise and epistemic justice, are central in conceptualising an inclusive workplace environment for neurodivergent teachers. Across the available literature, neurodivergent teachers share the importance of having agentic roles in schools in terms of supporting learners, developing inclusive cultures and increasing neurodiversity-related competencies. In particular, agency and autonomy for neurodivergent teachers in classrooms and teaching spaces is considered a key factor in positive school experiences (O'Neill and Kenny, 2023; Wharmby, 2022).

Relationships

Positive relationships that foster a sense of belonging are considered foundational in creating inclusive school environments (Goodall, 2020; Nind et al., 2022; Noddings, 1984). How relationships influence the workplace experiences of neurodivergent teachers is explored in the literature (O'Neill and Kenny, 2023; Wood et al., 2022a).

> *I've always felt I'll be accepted as some squished version of myself.*
>
> Deirdre

This statement from a neurodivergent teacher exemplifies that not all school-based relationships are nurturing. However, when relationships form in an inclusive and supportive school culture there are benefits for all. For example, the positive impact of neurodivergent teachers on the experiences of learners is a key finding across all the literature. Furthermore, research suggests that positive relationships contribute to self-efficacy and job satisfaction for teachers with autism, creating a more positive learning environment for all.

Nature

Interest in the impact of nature on neurodivergent wellbeing is gaining traction (Friedman et al., 2024; Loy-Ashe, 2023). In terms of education, it is posited that the benefits of using outdoor spaces for all learners may also address the more specific environmental and regulation needs of neurodivergent learners (Mogren, 2019). It is of relevance to this chapter that outdoor school spaces play a significant role in the experiences of many teachers with autism (O'Neill and Kenny, 2023). For example, one teacher participant in this research conceptualises the '*ideal school*' as one that uses outdoor learning environments, as nature counteracts the '*feeling of overload and that feeling of desk, chair and book*'.

Inclusion and intersectionality

It is essential that school leaders and all staff and stakeholders working in collaboration towards more inclusive workplace environments for neurodivergent teachers have an explicitly shared understanding of what is meant by inclusion. Inclusion as a concept, although broadly understood, is nevertheless difficult to define (Graham et al., 2024; Hodkinson and Vickerman, 2016). This chapter is written with an understanding of inclusion framed explicitly by a neurodiversity-affirmative focus. It is only by sharing our understanding of inclusion that we can take the next steps and transform ideals that are abstract and aspirational to operational actions and measurable impact. Here, the LEARNING Framework offers an explicit scaffold to shape educational collaborations and inclusive learning environments. It is also important on an individual level to reflect on what inclusion means to you as a leader and in the specific context of your school. Critically examining inclusion through the lens of the experiences of marginalised communities in your school, although potentially challenging, can be transformative. This reflective perspective also directly benefits neurodivergent teachers. Inclusion is broader than neurodiversity alone and the experiences of neurodivergent teachers often intersect with other dimensions of inclusion and diversity, including gender, culture and health.

Neurodiversity-informed

It might seem too obvious to state that any attempts to support neurodivergent teachers should be informed by the neurodiversity paradigm (Walker, 2021). However, with the emergence of phenomena like *neurodiversity-lite*, where the principles of the paradigm are misunderstood and sometimes even misappropriated, it is important to explicitly outline what being *neurodiversity-informed* looks like in operation.

To be neurodiversity-informed in one's approach requires a combination of knowledge, skills and disposition. The lists below share information about what neurodiversity is and also what it is not. Readers might find it useful to reflect on the bullet points below and use this to critically appraise your neurodiversity-related knowledge.

Neurodiversity:

- is naturally occurring in humankind;
- is a similar concept to biodiversity;
- recognises that the experience of neurominority groups shares similarities with the experiences of other minority groups in society;
- as a paradigm provides us with a shared framework and language to further understand all kinds of body-minds;
- as a paradigm is informed by the lived experience and tacit knowledge of neurodivergent individuals.

Neurodiversity is not:

- a concept that preferences some types of body-minds over others;
- an individual descriptor; we collectively are neurodiverse. For example, it is correct to refer to a neurodiverse school community. The phrase neurodiverse learner is incorrect;
- a movement synonymous with a strengths-based approach; it is a value-neutral occurrence;
- similar to neurodiversity-lite and performative neurodiversity; a neurodiversity-informed approach is different.

School leaders who consistently work towards being neurodiversity-informed and have a willingness to learn from the lived experiences of neurodivergent members of the school community demonstrate an understanding of the psychological safety needed for a learning environment to be truly inclusive (Berger et al., 2021; Edmondson, 1999).

Goals

In developing inclusive practices, it is helpful for school leaders to set, work towards and evaluate collaboratively-agreed goals. Working towards meaningful and specific goals keeps a sense of forward momentum and purpose when looking to recruit, support and nurture neurodivergent teachers. Moreover, clearly-defined goals help with collective accountability and responsibility. Goals, especially when communicated effectively, make efforts more formal and transparent. In the context of the LEARNING Framework, goals are broadly synonymous with phenomena like key performance indicators or statements of practice, intentions, standards, or calibrating matrixes. Scaffolds beyond the LEARNING Framework can also be useful in considering goals. For example, a broader framework like the United Nations Sustainable Goals for Development (United Nations, 2015) offers effective tools to develop achievable goals in designing and developing inclusive experiences for neurodivergent teachers.

Benefits

The benefit of using a framework like this is that it combines universal approaches to inclusion and incorporates the specificity that neurodivergent members of the school community might need. Although approaches like universal design benefit all, neurodivergent members of the school community will benefit from the more neurodiversity-focused sections above and explored further in the key areas section below.

The framework outlines the key areas to focus on to better support neurodivergent teachers. In addition to the key components of the framework other specific areas include:

- clear and transparent communication;
- advance notice of change and transitions;
- dedicated teaching space;
- dedicated quiet and calm rest area;
- neurodivergent-to-neurodivergent support. This could be peer-support, mentoring, coaching, community practice or ideally a combination of these;
- flexibility that incorporates an understanding of neurodivergent ways of being (for example, roster supervision in less busy areas of the school, understanding why a member of staff might find a busy staffroom overwhelming, non-mandatory attendance at social functions);
- energy levels. The energy levels of neurodivergent teachers are likely to oscillate and might be further impacted by intersecting chronic conditions.

IMPLEMENTATION: APPROACHES AND CHALLENGES

In terms of implementation, context is key. The approaches and challenges for each reader will be heterogeneous and will need to be informed by contextual variables like lived and professional experience, school-wide neurodiversity-related skills, knowledge and attitudes. Moreover, the capacity, willingness and motivation of key stakeholders to make changes in practice, procedure and policy is foundational to successful implementation. Nonetheless, an awareness of some widely effective approaches as well as common barriers and challenges is helpful. Therefore, it might be an effective exercise to critically engage with some general approaches and challenges outlined below and reflect on how these relate to your school setting.

Consider approaches that:

- use inclusive frameworks;
- are evidence informed;
- include neurodivergent expertise;
- make use of reflective practice;
- have built-in evaluative tools;
- are iterative and collaborative.

Barriers and challenges to consider:

- your motivation to become more neurodiversity informed;
- readiness at personal and school level to become more neurodiversity informed;
- initiative overload: how many change processes are being implemented by your school at present?
- how will being more cognisant of neurodivergent staff align with current school culture, values, mission and vision?
- how safe and inclusive is the school environment currently for neurodivergent teachers who might wish to disclose their neurotype?

Sometimes frameworks can help to structure our reflective practice. Consider using the LEARNING Framework or another framework like Rolfe's reflective framework (2002) to structure and record your baseline, decide on next steps and evaluate progress. Often, statements of practice and key performance indicators can help to capture current practice and illuminate the next steps necessary to calibrate to higher statements of practice. Furthermore, in my experience, using a structured framework facilitates and focuses collaborative reflection. Finally, a coaching model like the GROW model is ideal to guide reflective practice as it relates to this topic (Whitmore, 1996).

Goal

What is the goal?

Reality

What is the current reality?

Options

What options (including resources, access to support and training) do I have?

Will/way forward

What is my willingness to implement this change process? Have I planned and consulted enough to visualise a way forward in this?

A structured approach might not suit every reflective practitioner. The questions that follow might suit those who prefer a less structured and more open-ended approach to reflection.

1. Where do you think your school and your professional practice is currently in relation to inclusivity and neurodiversity-affirmative practices?
2. How do you know this? What is the evidence?
3. What is the next small action you can take to improve current practice?

CONCLUSION

The LEARNING Framework can support leaders with recruiting, supporting and retaining neurodivergent teaching staff. Operationalising the practical steps shared in this chapter will help you to contribute to the development of school cultures where neurodivergent teachers can thrive and flourish. By working towards this specific aim, it is possible to further develop optimal conditions for more broadly diverse and inclusive staff teams. The content is intentionally shared in a way to be of benefit to those new to the profession while enabling all staff members to progress in their journey towards becoming neurodiversity-informed educators. Specifically, it lends support to school leaders who wish to address the barriers that neurodivergent individuals might face in becoming teachers and progressing into leadership positions.

FURTHER LEARNING

- Fletcher Watson (2022) Neurodiversity-affirmative Education. CRAE Annual Lecture. Available at: www.youtube.com/watch?v=9iUHHmHftQs (accessed: 26 January 2025).

  This is a solid starting point for any educator wishing to become more neurodiversity-informed. Professor Sue Fletcher Watson shares an accurate and easy to understand overview of neurodiversity and the neurodiversity paradigm. Furthermore, how neurodiversity relates to education is explored in a clear and practical fashion. A highly recommended watch!

- Autistic School Staff Project (2025) Available at: www.autisticschoolstaffproject.com (accessed 26 January 2025).

    This website hosts a wide range of resources including webinars, articles and blog entries by autistic school staff. The project has also published a handbook comprising of chapters written by autistic teachers (Wood et al., 2022b).

- Keane E., Heinz M. and McDaid R. (2023) *Diversifying the Teaching Profession: Dimensions, Dilemmas and Directions for the Future.* London: Taylor & Francis.

    This open access book, although wider in focus, is an essential read for those wishing to understand the key factors worthy of consideration when seeking to further diversify the teaching profession.

REFERENCES

Autistic School Staff Project (2025) Available at: www.autisticschoolstaffproject.com (accessed: 26 January 2025).

Baird, A. (2020) Teaching while autistic: constructions of disability, performativity, and identity. *Ought: The Journal of Autistic Culture*, 2(1), 36–45. doi:10.9707/2833-1508.1040

Berger, E., D'Souza, L. and Miko, A. (2021) School-based interventions for childhood trauma and autism spectrum disorder: a narrative review. *The Educational and Developmental Psychologist*, 38(2), 186–93.

Botha, M. (2021) Academic, activist, or advocate? Angry, entangled, and emerging: a critical reflection on autism knowledge production. *Frontiers in Psychology*, 4196. doi: https://doi.org/10.3389/fpsyg.2021.727542

Burns, E. and Bell, S. (2011) Narrative construction of professional teacher identity of teachers with dyslexia. *Teaching and Teacher Education*, 27(5), 952–60. doi: https://doi.org/10.1016/j.tate.2011.03.007

Bury, S.M., Jellett, R., Haschek, A., Wenzel, M., Hedley, D., and Spoor, J.R. (2023) Understanding language preference: autism knowledge, experience of stigma and autism identity. *Autism*, 27(6), 1588–600. doi: https://doi.org/10.1177/136236132211423

Catala, A., Faucher, L. and Poirier, P. (2021) Autism, epistemic injustice, and epistemic disablement: a relational account of epistemic agency. *Synthese*, 199(3–4), 9013–39. doi: https://doi.org/10.1007/s11229-021-03192-7

Edmondson, A. (1999) Psychological safety and learning behavior in work teams. *Administrative Science Quarterly*, 44(2), 350–83.

Fletcher-Watson, S. (2022) *Neurodiversity-affirmative Education.* CRAE Annual Lecture. Available at: www.youtube.com/watch?v=9iUHHmHftQs (accessed: 26 January 2025).

Friedman, S.A., Morrison, S. and Shibata, A. (2024) Practitioner perspectives on nature-based learning for autistic children. *Journal of Environmental Education*, 1–15. doi: https://doi.org/10.1080/00958964.2024.2401785

Goodall, C. (2020) Inclusion is a feeling, not a place: a qualitative study exploring autistic young people's conceptualisations of inclusion. *International Journal of Inclusive Education*, 24(12), 1285–310. doi: https://doi.org/10.1080/13603116.2018.1523475

Graham, L.J. (2024) What is inclusion ... and what is it not? In L.J. Graham (ed.), *Inclusive Education for the 21st Century*. London: Routledge, pp. 18–37.

Harris, J. (2024) *How I Manage My ADHD as a Teacher*. Available at: https://set.et-foundation.co.uk/ (accessed: 26 January 2025).

Hodkinson, A. and Vickerman, P. (2016) *Inclusion: Defining Definitions*. London: Routledge, pp. 7–13.

Kantawala, A. (2023) Confluence of pedagogical frameworks: crafting a blueprint for inspired learning. *Art Education*, 76(5) 4–7. doi: https://doi.org/10.1080/00043125.2023.2261829

Keane, E., Heinz, M. and McDaid, R. (2023) *Diversifying the Teaching Profession: Dimensions, Dilemmas and Directions for the Future*. London: Taylor & Francis.

Kefallinou, A., Symeonidou, S. and Meijer, C.J. (2020) Understanding the value of inclusive education and its implementation: a review of the literature. *Prospects*, 49(3), 135–52. doi: https://doi.org/10.1007/s11125-020-09500-2

Lawrence, C. (2019) 'I can be a role model for autistic pupils': investigating the voice of the autistic teacher. *Teacher Education Advancement Network Journal*, 11(2), 50–8.

Loy-Ashe, T. (2023) Neurodivergence is also an LGBTQ+ topic: making space for 'neuro-queering' in the outdoors. *Parks Stewardship Forum*, 39(2). doi: https://doi.org/10.5070/P539260972

Mogren, A. (2019) Guiding principles of transformative education for sustainable development in local school organisations: investigating whole school approaches through a school improvement lens (doctoral dissertation, Karlstad University). Available at: www.researchgate.net/publication/338711490_Guiding_Principles_of_Transformative_Education_for_Sustainable_Development_in_Local_School_Organisations_Investigating_Whole_School_Approaches_through_a_School_Improvement_Lens (accessed: 20 May 2025).

Montero, C.S., Pope, N., Rötkönen, E. and Sutine, E. (2023) A systematic review of social classroom climate in online and technology-enhanced learning environments in primary and secondary school. *Education and Information Technologies*, 29, 2009–42. doi: https://doi.org/10.1007/s10639-023-11705-9

Nind, M., Köpfer, A. and Lemmer, K. (2022) Children's spaces of belonging in schools: bringing theories and stakeholder perspectives into dialogue. *International Journal of Inclusive Education*, 29(2), 210–22. doi: https://doi.org/10.1080/13603116.2022.2073061

Noddings, N. (1984) *Caring: A Feminine Approach to Ethics and Moral Education*. Berkeley: University of California Press.

O'Neill, C. (2024) *An Inclusive School Culture: Webinar with Inclusion Ireland*. Available at: www.youtube.com/watch?v=OTSeR-uL6kc (accessed: 26 January 2025)

O'Neill, C. and Kenny, N. (2023) 'I saw things through a different lens …': an interpretative phenomenological study of the experiences of autistic teachers in the Irish education system. *Education Sciences*, 13(7), 670. doi: https://doi.org/10.3390/educsci13070670

Riddick, B. (2003) Experiences of teachers and trainee teachers who are dyslexic. *International Journal of Inclusive Education*, 7(4), 389–402. doi: https://doi.org/10.1080/1360311032000110945

Rolfe, G. (2002) Reflective practice: where now? *Nurse Education in Practice*, 2(1), 21–9. doi: https://doi.org/10.1054/nepr.2002.0047

Romualdez, A.M., Walker, Z. and Remington, A. (2021) Autistic adults' experiences of diagnostic disclosure in the workplace: decision-making and factors associated with outcomes. *Autism and Developmental Language Impairments*, 6, 23969415211022955.

United Nations (2015) The United Nations Sustainable Development Goals. New York. Available at: https://sdgs.un.org/goals (accessed: 1 January 2024).

Walker, N. (2021) *Neuroqueer Heresies: Notes on The Neurodiversity Paradigm, Autistic Empowerment, and Postnormal Possibilities*. Berkeley, CA: Autonomous Press.

Wharmby, P. (2022) Special interests and their role in keeping the teacher in the classroom. In R. Wood, R. Moyse, L. Crane, F. Happé and A. Morrison (eds), *Learning from Autistic Teachers: How to be a Neurodiversity-Inclusive School*. London: Jessica Kingsley, pp. 29–43.

Whitmore, J. (1996) *Coaching for Performance*. London: N. Brealey.

Wood, R., Crane, L., Happé, F. and Moyse, R. (2022a) Learning from autistic teachers: lessons about change in an era of COVID-19. *Educational Review*, 76(5), 1209–231. doi: https://doi.org/10.1080/00131911.2022.2103521

Wood, R., Moyse, R., Crane, L., Happé, F. and Morrison, A. (eds) (2022b) *Learning from Autistic Teachers: How to be a Neurodiversity-Inclusive School*. London: Jessica Kingsley.

7

RECRUITING AND RETAINING LGBTQ+ TEACHERS THROUGH INCLUSIVE LEADERSHIP

PROFESSOR CATHERINE LEE

INTRODUCTION

Ensuring an inclusive and diverse teaching workforce is vital for fostering equitable educational environments in the UK. Despite legislative advancements and increased awareness of LGBTQ+ rights, the approximately 50,000 LGBTQ+ teachers in the UK continue to face significant barriers in recruitment, retention and professional progression. From the legacy of Section 28 to present-day discrimination and cultural challenges, many LGBTQ+ educators struggle with authenticity in their professional lives. This chapter explores the historical and contemporary barriers LGBTQ+ teachers face, examines strategies to promote LGBTQ+ inclusivity in educational settings and highlights the role of leadership development in creating positive change.

HISTORICAL CHALLENGES FOR LGBTQ+ TEACHERS

LGBTQ+ educators in the UK have long experienced systemic barriers to authenticity and professional growth. The introduction of Section 28 (1988–2003), which prohibited local authorities from 'promoting homosexuality' or teaching 'the acceptability of homosexuality as a pretended family relationship' in schools, had a profound impact on the teachers and LGBTQ+ students educated during that era (Lee, 2023). The legacy of Section 28 for LGBTQ+ teachers in the UK remains deeply embedded in the fabric of the education system, shaping professional identities, career trajectories and school cultures. While it no longer holds legal weight, its ideological and emotional impact continues to influence how LGBTQ+ teachers navigate their professional and personal lives within schools.

Many LGBTQ+ educators who worked during the era of the legislation internalised the message that their identities were incompatible with their professional roles. The widespread fear of being outed, whether through casual conversation or in the context of classroom discussions, led to self-censorship and isolation. This reluctance to be open about one's identity persisted even after the law was repealed, with many teachers continuing to feel that disclosure could jeopardise their careers or lead to professional stagnation (Lee, 2019). Lee notes that LGBTQ+ teachers who experienced the restrictions of the legislation often struggle with what she terms the inherited closet, wherein the professional norms established during that period continue to shape how LGBTQ+ teachers and students present themselves in school settings today. Additionally, the absence of affirmative LGBTQ+ representation in schools during the Section 28 era meant that younger educators who entered the profession in the post-repeal years had few role models to look up to.

A generational divide that often exists in schools between teachers who experienced Section 28 and those who entered the profession afterward has resulted in varying levels of confidence in discussing LGBTQ+ issues. Younger LGBTQ+ teachers often find themselves challenging the inherited caution of their older colleagues, who learned to navigate an education system that was, for many years, institutionally hostile towards them.

Despite the legal advancements in LGBTQ+ rights in the UK, the legacy of Section 28 manifests in the hesitancy many schools still exhibit when addressing LGBTQ+ issues. Some educators remain concerned that parental backlash or conservative governing bodies may challenge their professional credibility if they are open about their identities, leading to ongoing workplace insecurity. Baker (2022) has noted that the historical precedent set by Section 28 has contributed to a continued reluctance among some school leaders to fully embrace LGBTQ+ inclusivity, fearing controversy or negative attention.

The psychological impact of Section 28 extends beyond professional concerns and into personal well-being. LGBTQ+ teachers who experienced its enforcement frequently report higher levels of anxiety and imposter syndrome, stemming from years of working in environments where their identities were framed as inappropriate or unacceptable. Lecuyer (2025) highlighted how the enforced invisibility of LGBTQ+ educators under Section 28 has contributed to a lingering culture of silence, where many teachers still feel uncertain about whether they will be fully accepted within their school communities.

BARRIERS TO THE RECRUITMENT OF LGBTQ+ TEACHERS

The recruitment of LGBTQ+ teachers in the UK can be hindered by various factors, including discrimination during the recruitment process, a lack of visible LGBTQ+ role models in schools and fears of hostility from colleagues, students or parents. Many LGBTQ+ teacher candidates are reluctant to apply for positions due to uncertainty about the inclusivity of school environments.

While the Equality Act 2010 offers legal protections against discrimination based on sexual orientation and gender identity, the lived experiences of many LGBTQ+ educators suggest that inclusion within schools is far from guaranteed. Deep-rooted hetero and cis normative assumptions, workplace discrimination and a lack of visible LGBTQ+ role models continue to shape the professional trajectories of LGBTQ+ teachers, making their full participation in school communities more challenging than that of their counterparts. These barriers exist at multiple levels and start with recruitment. Schools can do a great deal to signal their LGBTQ+ inclusivity to candidates at interview. An invitation letter or email with a header or footer proclaiming the school has a achieved an LGBTQ+ inclusion kite mark is a good start. Rainbow flags, lanyards and displays also set an inclusive tone. LGBTQ+ inclusive policies, staff diversity statements and participation in LGBTQ+ awareness events such as Pride and LGBTQ+ History Month can help signal to applicants that a school is an inclusive workplace.

The intersection of LGBTQ+ identities with other aspects of identity, such as race, disability and religious affiliation, can further compound barriers to inclusion. Research by Bergerson et al. (2018) indicates that LGBTQ+ teachers from minority ethnic backgrounds often experience additional layers of exclusion, as they navigate both racialised and heteronormative expectations within school cultures. The compounding effects of multiple marginalised identities mean that these teachers often have to contend with additional biases and stereotypes that further alienate them in their school or education setting.

Despite challenges, there have been promising developments in recent years aimed at addressing the barriers LGBTQ+ teachers face. Organisations such as Stonewall, Courageous Leaders and Pride and Progress advocate for greater LGBTQ+ visibility in education and have worked to support LGBTQ+ teachers through professional networks. Schools that have actively implemented inclusion policies, professional development initiatives and LGBTQ+ staff networks have demonstrated that change is possible when there is institutional commitment.

However, inclusion cannot be left to individual schools or LGBTQ+ teachers or their motivated allies; it requires systemic change across the whole setting and a commitment from all stakeholders with clear policies and guidance to drive positive cultural change.

CREATING AN LGBTQ+ INCLUSIVE EDUCATIONAL SETTING

School leaders play a crucial role in shaping the culture of educational institutions and ensuring that LGBTQ+ teachers feel valued, supported and safe. Creating an inclusive school culture for LGBTQ+ teachers requires a proactive and intentional approach that goes beyond compliance to foster an environment where all educators can thrive. One of the most effective ways school leaders can create an inclusive culture is by embedding LGBTQ+ inclusion into the school's core values and policies. Research by Johnson (2023) highlights that truly inclusive schools explicitly state their commitment to LGBTQ+ inclusion in policies and have mission statements creating a safer and more welcoming environment for staff. Leaders who openly advocate for LGBTQ+ rights within the school community send a strong message that inclusivity is not optional, but a fundamental part of the school's ethos (Brett, 2024).

Training and professional development are also critical in fostering an inclusive school culture. Many teachers and staff members, including those in leadership positions, have received little to no formal training on LGBTQ+ inclusion, which can lead to uncertainty or reluctance in addressing discrimination (Sadowski, 2020). School leaders must integrate LGBTQ+ inclusion into CPD so that stakeholders can challenge unconscious bias and have the language and strategies to support LGBTQ+ colleagues, students and LGBTQ+ parents effectively (Markland, 2021). By integrating LGBTQ+ inclusion into wider diversity and equity training, school leaders can ensure that it becomes a natural and embedded part of professional development rather than an add-on or afterthought.

The visibility of LGBTQ+ teachers within the school is another important aspect of creating an inclusive culture. Schools where LGBTQ+ teachers feel comfortable being open about their identities tend to foster stronger professional relationships and higher job satisfaction (Lee, 2019). However, many LGBTQ+ teachers remain hesitant to be visible due to fears of discrimination or career stagnation. School leaders must actively challenge this culture of silence by ensuring that LGBTQ+ teachers are represented in decision-making processes and professional networks. Creating opportunities for LGBTQ+ teachers to engage in mentorship programmes, either within the school or through external organisations like Courageous Leaders, Pride and Progress or Pride in Leadership, can help provide the support and encouragement needed for career progression (Kimmel et al., 2021).

Ultimately, school leaders who take a holistic and committed approach to LGBTQ+ inclusion create educational environments where all staff members, regardless of their identities, feel empowered to be themselves. By embedding LGBTQ+ inclusivity into policy, training, visibility and community engagement, schools move beyond tokenism to foster a truly inclusive culture where LGBTQ+ teachers can thrive professionally as their authentic selves.

PROMOTING AN LGBTQ+ INCLUSIVE CURRICULUM

A truly inclusive educational setting must also extend to the curriculum. Representation matters and integrating LGBTQ+ themes into the curriculum normalises diverse identities while challenging hetero and cis normative narratives. This can include incorporating LGBTQ+ history, literature and social studies into lesson plans, using gender-inclusive language in teaching materials and ensuring that LGBTQ+ identities are visible in classroom displays and discussions. Ofsted's guidance on personal, social, health and economic (PSHE) education encourages schools to adopt a more inclusive approach, ensuring that students are educated about diverse identities from an early age.

LGBTQ+ identities, histories and experiences should ideally be integrated across subject areas rather than treated as isolated topics. This helps to normalise diverse identities rather than presenting them as deviations from a heteronormative standard. For example, in English literature, teachers can introduce texts by LGBTQ+ authors or analyse characters and themes related to gender and sexuality. William Shakespeare's sonnets, for example are subject to analysis regarding potential queer subtexts, particularly *Fair Youth*, widely believed to express love or admiration for a young man. Oscar Wilde's work explores themes of identity, secrecy and social hypocrisy and his life was marked by persecution, but his wit and critique of Victorian morality continue to resonate in contemporary discussions of LGBTQ+ identity. Virginia Woolf's *Orlando* (1928) chronicles the life of the protagonist who changes sex over centuries and Woolf's relationship with Vita Sackville-West, an openly bisexual writer, influenced this novel's exploration of gender and identity.

One of the most well-known historical figures associated with both education and LGBTQ+ identity is Alan Turing. Turing's work as a mathematician and computer scientist profoundly influenced modern education in STEM fields. His contributions during World War II, particularly in breaking the German Enigma code, were crucial to the Allied victory. However, Turing was criminally prosecuted for his homosexuality in 1952, subjected to chemical castration and died under tragic circumstances. Exploring the lives of Turing and other LGBTQ+ historical figures within an LGBTQ+ inclusive curriculum helps to increase awareness and develop a cultural understanding of prejudice.

For younger students, there are a host of LGBTQ+ inclusive age-appropriate resources that focus on celebrating difference. The No Outsiders programme is one example of this where storybooks are used to introduce and discuss various aspects of diversity, including race, religion, gender identity, disability and sexual orientation. Diverse characters prepare children for life in modern Britain by teaching them to respect and embrace differences.

THE IMPORTANCE OF LGBTQ+ ROLE MODELS

LGBTQ+ teachers serve as vital role models for students and colleagues alike. The visibility of LGBTQ+ educators helps challenge stereotypes, create safe spaces for LGBTQ+ students and foster a culture of acceptance. Schools should actively celebrate LGBTQ+ teachers by recognising their contributions, supporting LGBTQ+ teacher-led initiatives and marking key dates such as LGBTQ+ History Month and Pride celebrations.

The choice of whether to be out in the school workplace ultimately belongs to the LGBTQ+ teacher. They must not be coerced into coming out, but they should be fully supported and empowered to do so if they choose. Schools must create environments where LGBTQ+ teachers feel safe, valued and protected so that coming out is an option rather than an obligation. Mary Lou Rasmussen's 'The problem of coming out' (2004) critically examines the LGBTQ+ teacher visibility, particularly the assumption that coming out is always necessary. Rasmussen argues that the expectation to disclose one's LGBTQ+ identity reinforces heteronormative structures rather than dismantling them, as it positions LGBTQ+ identities as something that must be declared in order to be recognised. Additionally, the concept of coming out is not always empowering for everyone. Rasmussen (2004) critiques the idea that LGBTQ+ teachers must always disclose their identities in order to be 'authentic'. She argues that this framework reinforces heteronormative assumptions, making LGBTQ+ people feel as if their identities are only valid when publicly declared. Some LGBTQ+ teachers may not see their sexual orientation or gender identity as relevant to their professional role, preferring to maintain privacy in the workplace. This choice should be respected, as forcing disclosure can be as exclusionary as outright discrimination.

PROTECTING LGBTQ+ TEACHERS FROM CONSERVATIVE PARENTS AND GOVERNORS

Discrimination and prejudice from conservative parents and governing bodies poses a significant challenge to LGBTQ+ inclusion in schools. Some parents object to LGBTQ+ representation in the curriculum, while others challenge LGBTQ+ teachers' visibility in schools, concerned that an LGBTQ+ teacher's own identity might promote or encourage children to become LGBTQ+ themselves. School leaders must navigate these tensions carefully, ensuring that their policies align with the Equality Act 2010, protecting LGBTQ+ staff from discrimination. Engaging in open dialogue with parents, offering educational resources on LGBTQ+ inclusion and demonstrating that diversity is an essential part of school values can help mitigate parental opposition (Payne and Smith, 2012).

School governors or trustees often bring a more conservative stance on LGBTQ+ teacher identities to these voluntary roles, and this can be challenging for school leaders to navigate. Regular mandatory training on LGBTQ+ inclusivity is paramount as is the opportunity for regular school visits so that governors and trustees can see inclusivity in action.

Andrew Moffat, a British educator and the creator of the No Outsiders programme, faced significant backlash from conservative parents, particularly within Muslim communities in Birmingham, over his efforts to promote LGBTQ+ inclusion in schools. The controversy erupted at Parkfield Community School, where Moffat served as Assistant Headteacher, and sparked a national debate about how LGBTQ+ topics should be addressed in primary education. The No Outsiders programme was designed to align with the Equality Act 2010, which mandates that schools teach about different forms of discrimination and promote respect for all individuals. However, some parents, predominantly from religious and conservative backgrounds, argued that discussing LGBTQ+ issues with young children was inappropriate and contradicted their religious beliefs. The opposition intensified in early 2019, when groups of parents began organising protests outside Parkfield Community School. These protests involved hundreds of parents withdrawing their children from classes in a coordinated effort to pressure the school into halting LGBTQ+ inclusivity lessons. The protests gained media attention and highlighted broader tensions between LGBTQ+ rights and religious freedoms in the UK education system. Moffat, who is gay, became the personal target of hostile rhetoric and allegations. Some parents distributed leaflets and WhatsApp messages accusing him of having an agenda to 'indoctrinate' children. The protests escalated to the point where Moffat received death threats and had to step back from leading the programme at Parkfield, although No Outsiders was later reinstated with modifications to address parental concerns. Moffatt's experience underscores the challenges faced by LGBTQ+ educators working to implement LGBTQ+ inclusive policies and highlights the importance of supportive leaders and governing bodies at challenging times for LGBTQ+ teachers.

PHASE-SPECIFIC LGBTQ+ TEACHER INCLUSION

Of course, effective LGBTQ+ teacher inclusion differs in each phase of compulsory education. The early years of education provide a crucial foundation for inclusivity. LGBTQ+ inclusion at this stage is often met with resistance due to misconceptions that discussions of gender and sexuality are inappropriate for young children. However, research shows that early exposure to diverse family structures and inclusive language helps foster empathy and acceptance from an early age (Bradbury, 2021). Schools and nurseries should ensure that classroom materials reflect diverse families, provide staff training on inclusive teaching and incorporate LGBTQ+ representation in discussions about identity and relationships.

Primary education shapes children's understanding of diversity. Inclusive policies in primary schools should ensure that LGBTQ+ families and identities are acknowledged in school culture and curricula. Strategies such as using inclusive storybooks, celebrating diverse family structures and training teachers to challenge gender stereotypes contribute to creating an affirming school environment. Additionally, embedding LGBTQ+ inclusion in school policies ensures that it is not dependent on individual teacher advocacy, but is part of the broader educational ethos.

Secondary schools present unique opportunities and challenges for LGBTQ+ inclusion. At this stage, students are increasingly aware of issues related to identity and discrimination.

Schools must actively integrate LGBTQ+ themes into subjects such as history, literature and citizenship education to normalise diversity. LGBTQ+ student Pride groups provide safe spaces for students to discuss their identities and experiences. Additionally, staff training on how to support LGBTQ+ students and colleagues is crucial for ensuring that secondary schools remain safe and inclusive spaces.

RETAINING LGBTQ+ TEACHERS

Retaining LGBTQ+ teachers requires a multifaceted approach that addresses both structural and cultural barriers within schools. Many LGBTQ+ educators leave the profession due to workplace discrimination, lack of career progression and the emotional toll of navigating hetero and cis normative environments (Lee, 2019). However, LGBTQ+ teachers who feel safe and included in their school setting are likely to reward it with their loyalty. Research by Lee showed that teachers who are out at school are seven times more likely to stay than their heterosexual and cis-gendered counterparts (Lee, 2019).

One of the most effective ways to retain LGBTQ+ teachers is by fostering a visibly inclusive school culture. Explicit policies supporting LGBTQ+ inclusion, such as clear anti-discrimination protections, gender-neutral facilities and zero-tolerance policies for homophobia and transphobia are key. School leaders must ensure that inclusivity is not just a statement in policy documents, but is actively practised in the school workplace culture. Another key factor in retention is providing LGBTQ+ teachers with mentorship and professional development opportunities. Groups of schools can establish LGBTQ+ staff networks that offer peer support, opportunities for career progression and safe spaces for discussing education workplace challenges.

Schools must also address career progression barriers that disproportionately affect LGBTQ+ teachers. Research by Lee (2023) indicates that many LGBTQ+ educators experience a 'glass closet' in their careers, where they are either overlooked for promotion or feel that disclosing their identity will hinder their advancement or necessitate a level of visibility among parents that they are uncomfortable with. To counteract this, schools should ensure that promotion processes are equitable, using diverse interview panels and explicit statements encouraging LGBTQ+ applicants. Creating career pathways for LGBTQ+ teachers, including specific training and networking opportunities, can help foster a sense of belonging and career ambition.

Mental health and well-being support is essential for retaining LGBTQ+ teachers, many of whom experience higher levels of stress due to workplace discrimination or the emotional labour of self-censorship (Meyer, 2003). Schools should provide confidential mental health resources, access to employee assistance programmes and a culture where seeking support is normalised rather than stigmatised. By embedding these practices, schools can move beyond symbolic inclusivity and create genuinely supportive environments where LGBTQ+ teachers feel safe, respected and empowered to build long-term careers.

SUPPORTING LGBTQ+ TEACHERS TO BECOME SCHOOL LEADERS

The presence of LGBTQ+ leaders in schools can be a catalyst for LGBTQ+ inclusion. Encouraging LGBTQ+ teachers to take on leadership roles as their authentic selves fosters an environment where diversity is valued. Research also indicates that the challenges and adversities faced by LGBTQ+ teachers can equip them with unique skills and attributes that are highly beneficial in school leadership roles, particularly when they are able to be authentic in their professional environments (Lee, 2020). Authentic leadership involves a leader's self-awareness, encompassing an ongoing process of understanding their talents, strengths, purpose, core values, beliefs and desires. Authentic leadership emphasises relational transparency, characterised by open and honest communication and relationships with colleagues (Avolio and Gardner, 2005).

While much of the existing literature on authentic leadership originates from corporate contexts, these principles are applicable to educational settings. LGBTQ+ teachers often develop resilience and adaptability through navigating adversity, vigilance, marginalisation and uncertainty both within and beyond the school and environment. These experiences can cultivate attributes that predispose them to excel in school leadership positions. According to Lee (2020), key attributes identified in LGBTQ+ aspiring school leaders include:

- *inclusion*: having often experienced exclusion themselves, LGBTQ+ teachers are typically highly attuned to inclusive practices. They possess a heightened awareness of individuals on the margins of the school community and actively seek ways to ensure these individuals feel included. This empathy extends to students, parents and colleagues who may face marginalisation based on race, faith, or social class, fostering compassionate leadership;
- *adaptability*: accustomed to tolerating ambiguity, LGBTQ+ teachers often manage personal stress while maintaining professionalism. This ability to operate under pressure without revealing personal turmoil is invaluable in leadership roles, where safeguarding the school community from uncertainty or adversity is essential;
- *connectivity*: navigating predominantly heteronormative spaces, LGBTQ+ individuals are adept at identifying opportunities to connect with others, even those with whom they may not initially have much in common. This skill is crucial for school leaders working with diverse stakeholders across the school community;
- *communication*: LGBTQ+ school leaders who are open about their identities often experience more authentic relationships with colleagues. By sharing personal aspects of themselves, they build trust, encouraging candidness and fostering a supportive work environment;
- *intuition*: years of cautiously interacting with new individuals to protect themselves from potential discrimination often result in LGBTQ+ individuals developing excellent emotional intelligence. They become adept at reading situations and making quick, accurate judgements about others, skills that are beneficial in decision-making processes such as recruiting employees;

- *collaboration*: many LGBTQ+ individuals create families of choice, forming supportive networks that traditionally come from families of origin. This experience translates into the ability to foster a sense of belonging and collaboration within the school community, uniting stakeholders toward common goals;
- *courage*: LGBTQ+ teachers often exhibit courage and a willingness to take risks, such as applying for new positions despite potential homo or trans phobia in new work environments. Their visibility within schools challenges traditional norms and provides diverse role models for students.

The Courageous Leaders programme was the UK's first school leadership initiative for LGBTQ+ teachers. The programme enabled participants to focus on their development as authentic leaders, free from the need to manage their sexual, gender and professional identities separately. Supported by mentors, over 80 per cent of the 105 teachers participating in the programme secured their desired promotion within a year. Despite its success, the programme reached fewer than 0.01 per cent of the LGBTQ+ teacher population before its DfE funding ended. At a time when the average tenure for a headteacher in the UK is just three years, programmes like Courageous Leaders play a crucial role in enhancing the diversity of teacher leaders and fostering school cultures that allow teachers to be their authentic selves and thrive within the profession.

Ensuring the full inclusion of LGBTQ+ teachers within the UK education system is not just a matter of policy compliance, but a fundamental step towards fostering an equitable and enriching learning environment for all. The persistent impact of historical discrimination, coupled with contemporary barriers to recruitment, retention and leadership progression, underscores the urgent need for systemic change. Despite legal protections and advocacy efforts, many LGBTQ+ educators still navigate professional landscapes that demand self-censorship, resilience and adaptability in the face of adversity.

Creating genuinely inclusive schools requires more than symbolic gestures – it necessitates a cultural shift that embeds LGBTQ+ inclusion into every facet of the educational system. This means cultivating leadership pathways that embrace authenticity, developing supportive networks and ensuring that LGBTQ+ teachers feel empowered rather than marginalised in their professional environments. Schools must not only protect LGBTQ+ educators from discrimination, but also celebrate their presence as vital contributors to the educational community.

CONCLUSION

LGBTQ+ teachers serve as role models, advocates and catalysts for change, influencing both their colleagues and students. By fostering an education system where LGBTQ+ teachers can thrive, we create learning environments that reflect the diversity of society, encourage open dialogue and empower the next generation to embrace inclusivity. In inclusive schools,

LGBTQ+ teachers are not merely accommodated, but are actively supported and elevated in their careers. Leadership development programmes, inclusive policies and a commitment to genuine representation must be at the heart of this transformation. The future of education depends on the ability of schools to create spaces where every teacher, regardless of their identity, can bring their full, authentic self to their profession. Only then can we achieve a fully inclusive and representative teaching workforce that benefits us all.

FURTHER LEARNING

- Brett, A. and Brassington, J. (2023) *Pride and Progress: Making Schools LGBT+ Inclusive Spaces*. London: Sage.

    Pride and Progress is an essential guide for educators looking to foster LGBTQ+ inclusivity in schools. Drawing on insights from the Pride and Progress podcast, it combines theory, practical strategies and reflective exercises to help educators create safer, more accepting learning environments. With a reassuring approach, Brett and Brassington emphasise that discomfort is part of meaningful change, making this a must-read for those committed to building truly inclusive schools.

- Lee, C. (2020) *Courage in the Classroom: LGBT Teachers Share Their Stories*. London: Hachette.

    This is a powerful collection of accounts from LGBTQ+ educators about their experiences in schools. The book highlights the challenges, triumphs and resilience of LGBTQ+ teachers as they navigate issues of identity, inclusion and professional authenticity. It explores the impact of coming out in the workplace, the role of LGBTQ+ educators as role models and the systemic barriers they face in the education system. Through these personal narratives, the book sheds light on the importance of creating supportive, inclusive environments for both teachers and students.

REFERENCES

Avolio, B.J. and Gardner, W.L. (2005) Authentic leadership development: getting to the root of positive forms of leadership. *The Leadership Quarterly*, 16(3), 315–38.

Baker, P. (2022) *Outrageous! The Story of Section 28 and Britain's Battle for LGBT Education*. London: Reaktion.

Bergersen, M., Klar, S. and Schmitt, E. (2018) Intersectionality and engagement among the LGBTQ+ community. *Journal of Women, Politics and Policy*, 39(2), 196–219.

Bradbury A. (2021) *Ability, Inequality and Post-Pandemic Schools: Rethinking Contemporary Myths of Meritocracy*. Bristol: Policy Press.

Bradbury A. (2023) Working with LGBT+ parent-led families. In: Simmons H and Thompson P (Eds.) (2023) *Partnership with Parents in Early Childhood Today*. London: Sage, 74.

Brett, A. (2024) Under the spotlight: exploring the challenges and opportunities of being a visible LGBT+ teacher. *Sex Education*, 24(1), 61–75.

Johnson, B. (2023) Creating and sustaining LGBTQ+ inclusive communities of practice in UK primary schools: an interpretative phenomenological analysis. *Journal of LGBT Youth*, 20(3), 545–60.

Kimmel L., Lachlan L. and Guiden A. (2021) The Power of Teacher Diversity: Fostering Inclusive Conversations through Mentoring. Available at: https://files.eric.ed.gov/fulltext/ED615359.pdf (accessed: 23 May 2025).

Lecuyer, A. (2025) 20 years since Section 28: an examination of the non-mandatory status of LGBT curricular inclusion in English primary schools. *Sexualities*, 13634607251323064.

Lee, C. (2019) Fifteen years on: the legacy of section 28 for LGBT+ teachers in English schools. *Sex Education*, 19(6), 675–90.

Lee, C. (2020) Why LGBT teachers may make exceptional school leaders. *Frontiers in Sociology*, 5, 50.

Lee, C. (2023) *Pretended: Schools and Section 28: Historical, Cultural and Personal Perspectives*. Suffolk: John Catt.

Markland, B. (2021) What can teachers do to embed LGBTQ+ inclusive practices in schools? Doctoral dissertation, University of Southampton.

Meyer I.H. (2003) Prejudice, Social Stress, and Mental Health in Lesbian, Gay, and Bisexual Populations: Conceptual Issues and Research Evidence. *Psychological Bulletin*, 129(5), 674–697.

Payne, E. and Smith, M. (2012) Increasing competence and overcoming fear: a case for LGBTQ-inclusive multicultural teacher education. *Research and Support for Multicultural Education Course Requirements in Teacher Education in New York State*, 30–41.

Rasmussen, M.L. (2004) The problem of coming out. *Theory into Practice*, 43(2), 144–50.

Sadowski, M. (2020) *Safe is Not Enough: Better Schools for LGBTQ Students*. Cambridge, MA: Harvard Education Press.

PART 3
BUILDING SUPPORTIVE WORK ENVIRONMENTS
FOSTERING CAREER PROGRESSION FOR ALL

8

SUPPORTING TEACHER RETENTION AND CAREER PROGRESSION

FOSTERING EARLY CAREER TEACHER SELF-EFFICACY THROUGH REFLECTIVE PRACTICE AND PROFESSIONAL DEVELOPMENT

PROFESSOR TANYA OVENDEN-HOPE

INTRODUCTION

The education landscape in England faces a critical challenge: the significant and sustained attrition of early career teachers (ECTs) and its subsequent impact on education stability. As a school leader, you play a pivotal role in shaping the professional journey of ECTs and are therefore crucial to any plan for improving ECT retention. This chapter addresses how reflective practice and targeted professional development can foster self-efficacy, autonomy and job satisfaction among ECTs, ultimately improving retention rates and supporting long-term career progression. As a school leader, understanding both the systemic challenges and evidence-based solutions for ECT attrition will equip you to create school environments where new teachers not only survive, but also thrive. You will gain insights into creating supportive cultures, implementing effective mentoring, designing meaningful professional development and fostering reflective practice – all crucial elements in addressing the *great supply crisis* (Ovenden-Hope, 2023) in teaching. By adopting a holistic and nurturing approach to ECT support, you can contribute significantly to the stability of your school and the broader education system. By the end of this chapter, you will have gained a deeper understanding of the challenges faced by ECTs, the importance of reflective practice and professional development in building self-efficacy, autonomy and job satisfaction, and practical approaches to implement supportive structures within your school.

UNDERSTANDING THE TEACHER RETENTION CRISIS AND CAREER PROGRESSION

The education system in England faces significant challenges in retaining teachers, particularly those in the early stages of their careers. The most recent government data on the teaching workforce released in June 2024 (DfE, 2024b) reported that only 88.7 per cent of teachers who qualified in 2022 were still teaching one year after qualification. The three-year retention rate for ECTs had decreased to 74.1 per cent compared to previous years, with 25.9 per cent leaving the profession within three years. The five-year retention rate had also declined, with only 67.5 per cent of teachers remaining in the profession after five years. This indicates a concerning trend of a worsening long-term retention problem for teachers in England.

Teacher vacancies had also increased significantly in the DfE's 2024 workforce data (DfE, 2024b), more than doubling over the past three years. This challenge in teacher recruitment was matched by an increase in the number of temporarily filled posts, which had almost doubled in three years. In 2023 only 59 per cent of teachers expected to still be teaching in three years' time, a significant decrease from pre-pandemic figures of 74–7 per cent (Allen et al., 2023). There has also been a decline in senior leaders aspiring to become headteachers, with only 43 per cent expressing this ambition, down from 56 per cent pre-pandemic (Allen et al., 2023). The massive decline in the number of newly qualified entrants to the profession in 2023–4 (17,462) – the lowest since current records began in 2010 (Booth, 2024) – compounds the teacher supply issues to create a perfect storm for school leaders trying to maintain consistent, high-quality staffing for their schools.

The recruitment and retention crisis creates multiple challenges for education, and school leaders particularly. The constant cycle of recruitment, induction and development consumes significant resources and leadership capacity. More critically, research consistently demonstrates that teacher expertise develops over time, meaning that schools with high teacher turnover may struggle to build the pedagogical expertise necessary for sustained educational improvement (Cordingley et al., 2019). For pupils, teacher turnover can disrupt learning relationships and contribute to inconsistent educational experiences, particularly in 'educationally isolated' schools (Allen and Sims, 2018; Ovenden-Hope et al., 2022).

The causes of teacher attrition are complex, with several factors identified as being major contributors to the reasons for why teachers leave the profession. While pay is certainly one consideration, with evidence suggesting that local pay gaps between teaching and other professions can affect retention (McClean et al., 2024), evidence suggests that the pay issue is more nuanced (Sibieta, 2020). In many parts of England, competing occupations offer salaries that are over £5,000 (11 per cent) higher than teaching, particularly in areas around London (Fullard and Zuccollo, 2021). This financial disadvantage can make it difficult to both recruit and retain teachers. For ECTs, financial pressures often increase as they progress through their career, making this pay gap with other professions more pronounced.

In post-war Britain, teacher shortages were addressed by the government through a massive increase in pay to bring teaching salaries in line with other professions (Howson, 2020). However, societal expectations for working life have changed in the 21st century, with work–life balance and flexible working additional considerations alongside pay when choosing a career (Harland et al., 2023). These changed expectations of working conditions suggest that teacher pay, even if it were addressed by the government to establish parity with other professions, such a medicine or law, represents only one element in a complicated puzzle for teacher retention.

Teacher self-efficacy, defined as a teacher's belief in their ability to effectively manage classroom situations and impact student learning (Bandura, 2012), and satisfaction are crucial factors for teacher retention. Workload concerns, lack of professional autonomy, insufficient support and limited opportunities for growth all feature prominently when teachers discuss reasons for leaving the profession (Worth and Van den Brande, 2020) and are all connected to teacher self-efficacy and satisfaction. Understanding these multiple factors' role in teacher attrition, and specifically ECT attrition, is essential for developing comprehensive approaches to retention that address the full range of teacher needs and concerns.

THE EARLY CAREER FRAMEWORK: PROMISES AND REALITIES

The Early Career Framework (ECF), described as 'one of the most significant reforms to the teaching profession in a generation', outlines what ECTs should learn and practice at the start of their careers (DfE, 2019b, p. 4). The ECF became mandatory in state-funded schools in England in September 2021, a core reform of the Teacher Recruitment and Retention Strategy (DfE, 2019a), and was improved (following findings from a DfE review in 2023) and aligned with initial teacher training (ITT) in September 2025 to become part of the Initial Teacher Training and Early Career Framework (ITTECF) (DfE, 2024a). The ECF is funded by the government and provides ECTs with an entitlement to a two-year induction period, an increase of non-timetabled time for professional development and structured support, including a dedicated mentor to facilitate professional growth during this critical career phase. This recognition of the importance of professional development to an occupation is core to its professional status and offers affirmation of the professional status of teaching.

The ECF was intended to address several key challenges for teacher supply by increasing ECT retention, improving the quality of teaching and enhancing teacher job satisfaction (DfE, 2019b). The extended and structured approach to early career development acknowledged that teaching expertise develops over time and requires ongoing support. The emphasis on mentoring recognised the value of experiential knowledge transfer and the importance of professional dialogue in teacher development (Hobson et al., 2009). However, early evaluations, and the government's own review (Department for Education, 2024c) demonstrated limitations of the ECF for ECTs, mentors and schools (Ovenden-Hope and Kirkpatrick, 2024).

An evaluation of the ECF early roll-out commissioned by the Education Endowment Foundation (EEF) reported some benefits of the ECF that included 'an improvement in ECTs' teaching practice, self-efficacy, confidence, and job satisfaction' (Walker et al., 2024, p. 5). The ECF structure, and particularly the mentorship, was found to help schools create supportive environments for new teachers. However, the EEF also reported on the significant challenges faced by ECTs participating in the ECF, such as increased workload from the ECF programme with insufficient time to dedicate to this. Wider research on the ECF corroborates these findings (Ovenden-Hope and Kirkpatrick, 2024). The EEF report concluded that the ECF early roll-out 'did not have a significant impact on ECT retention in the state sector after two years of induction' and that it actually had 'a null effect on retention' (Walker et al., 2024, p. 5).

Structured support for ECTs is clearly important, but complex, and this complexity suggests that a framework working in isolation of the range of factors influencing ECT retention is not sufficient to address ECT attrition. As a school leader, you will have realised that your role extends beyond implementing the ECF as prescribed; for effective support of your ECTs you will have considered how to adapt and enhance the framework to meet the specific needs of your ECTs and your school context. To be effective the formal structure provided by the ECF requires enhancement through school-level initiatives that address the full range of factors influencing teacher satisfaction, self-efficacy and thereby retention.

THE EARLY CAREER TEACHER EXPERIENCE

The transition from initial teacher training to full-time teaching is often described as a period of 'reality shock' for many ECTs (Veenman, 1984). This phase is characterised by a complex interplay of challenges that can significantly impact a teacher's decision to remain in the profession. Some of the key issues faced by ECTs include:

1. Workload intensity
2. Classroom management difficulties
3. Adapting to school culture and policies
4. Balancing teaching responsibilities with personal life
5. Navigating relationships with colleagues and parents.

(Ovenden-Hope et al., 2020)

The experiences of ECTs during their first few years can be pivotal in shaping their long-term career trajectories (Hobson et al. 2009).

KEY FACTORS INFLUENCING ECT RETENTION AND PROGRESSION

It is during this critical early period that school leaders have the opportunity to intervene and provide targeted support to nurture new teachers to help them flourish and find satisfaction in their new career. In order to do this, it is vital to understand the key factors influencing ECT retention and progression.

SELF-EFFICACY

Self-efficacy, defined in this context as a teacher's belief in their ability to teach effectively (accomplish a task) and impact positively on student learning (succeed in a specific situation), emerges as a critical factor in teacher retention (Bandura, 2012). Drawing on social cognitive theory, self-efficacy influences how teachers approach challenges, their resilience in the face of setbacks and, ultimately, their decision to remain in the profession. For ECTs, developing self-efficacy is particularly crucial as they navigate the challenges of establishing themselves as 'teachers' and building the foundations of greater job satisfaction (Klassen and Chiu, 2011). However, self-efficacy often follows a U-shaped trajectory for ECTs, starting high with a sharp decline as challenges in classroom practice are experienced (Woolfolk Hoy and Burke Spero, 2005). Knowing this, school leaders can anticipate and put in place the additional support, or targeted interventions, required for ECTs to regain their professional confidence.

The ECF aims to support ECTs' development of self-efficacy through structured mentoring and professional development (DfE, 2019b). By providing a framework of evidence-informed practice and dedicated mentoring, it seeks to build ECTs' confidence in their teaching abilities. However, the framework alone is proving insufficient for developing the deep sense of self-efficacy and autonomy that supports long-term retention (Ovenden-Hope and Kirkpatrick, 2025). To truly foster self-efficacy and autonomy, ECTs need opportunities to experience success in their teaching, receive specific feedback that helps them attribute that success to their own efforts and abilities, observe colleagues who model effective practice and engage in authentic reflection on their development. They also need gradually increasing responsibilities and opportunities to make professional judgements, with appropriate support and guidance.

By intentionally designing experiences that build self-efficacy and autonomy, you can help ECTs develop the confidence, resilience and sense of professional identity that contribute to a long-term commitment to teaching. These qualities not only support retention, but also enhance the quality of teaching and, consequently, student learning in your school. Interventions that enhance ECT self-efficacy should therefore be a cornerstone for teacher retention strategies. Teachers with a strong sense of self-efficacy believe they can positively affect pupil learning and accept responsibility for motivating pupils and for improving their teaching skills (Tschannen-Moran and Hoy, 2001). Teacher self-efficacy also supports more positive relationships with colleagues, leaders and parents/carers (Zee and Koomen, 2016; Klassen and Tze, 2014). Self-efficacy creates a virtuous cycle in practice – as teachers witness their positive impact on students, their self-efficacy increases, which in turn enhances their teaching effectiveness and job satisfaction.

REFLECTIVE PRACTICE AND PROFESSIONAL DEVELOPMENT

> Reflective practice is understood as the process of learning through and from experience towards gaining new insights of self and/or practice.
>
> (Finlay, 2006, p. 1)

Reflective practice can serve as the cornerstone for the professional development of ECTs. When engaged with effectively, developing habits of reflective practice provides a mechanism for continuous improvement and professional growth. Effective reflective practice goes beyond simply thinking about what happened in a lesson, it involves a teacher's critical evaluation of their own practice. ECTs that are supported in becoming reflective practitioners (Schön, 1983) typically build resilience with which to face professional challenges and experience greater agency and autonomy (Farrell, 2016). For ECTs, engaging in structured reflective practice can have multiple professional benefits:

1. processing and making sense of challenging experiences;
2. identifying areas for improvement and setting professional goals;
3. developing a sense of agency and control over their professional growth;
4. building resilience by recognising progress and successes.

However, reflective practice is not without challenges, and these challenges must be understood to embed it into ECT development effectively. As a school leader your role in nurturing reflective practice in your school should be informed by the following considerations:

1. fostering reflective practice for ECTs (and all teachers) requires a safe environment, sustained support through meaningful structures for reflection, modelling of reflective approaches by colleagues across the school and making sure that reflections lead to actionable insights;
2. reflective practice can challenge and question accepted individual and school practices and can therefore make teachers engaged with reflective practice vulnerable; supporting teachers will remove this 'risk' and can support outcomes;
3. if not managed well, reflective practice can become a time-consuming and/or mechanical checklist of actions in and on practice. This must be avoided.

By embedding reflective practice within a supportive professional community, you can help ECTs develop the professional practices that will sustain them throughout their careers.

The ECF materials acknowledge the requirement for reflection in ECTs' professional development, which requires both the development of knowledge, understanding and skills ('learn that') and the application of what has been learned to practice ('learn how to'):

Learn that ... Reflective practice, supported by feedback from and observation of experienced colleagues, professional debate, and learning from educational research, is also likely to support improvement ... Learn how to ... Develop as a professional by: ... Reflecting on progress made, recognising strengths and weaknesses and identifying next steps for further improvement.

(DfE, 2019b, p. 24)

If supported effectively, these reflective moments provide opportunities for ECTs to deepen their understanding of teaching and learning.

Teachers engage in a wide range of professional development, from government-developed mandatory programmes – such as the ECF – to formal qualifications such as master's degrees and specific teaching qualifications like national professional qualifications (NPQs). Schools also use externally provided courses, training delivered by the senior leadership team and other teacher-led development, such as observing other teachers and visiting other schools. Professional development mostly takes place within the school, which differs from the norm several years ago and is likely a reflection of reduced resources and school governance structures (Pollard et al., 2024).

While some view this move to school-based development positively as it leverages and recognises staff expertise, there are different drivers to participate in professional development. Some are state-driven, some are school-driven and others are personally motivated (Pollard et al., 2024). The potential for positive impact from professional development depends on several factors, but particularly the quality, applicability to practice and sustained nature of the provision. School leaders must also recognise that professional development creates additional workload and should be designed and scheduled thoughtfully to avoid contributing to ECT stress and possibly attrition.

For ECTs, structured professional development that encourages reflection can significantly impact their self-efficacy, confidence, satisfaction and retention. The RETAIN programme, a pilot intervention designed to improved ECT retention funded by the EEF prior to the ECF, provides an example of effective ECT professional development that embeds evidence-informed reflective practice within its content and delivery (Ovenden-Hope et al., 2018). Using a combination of theoretical knowledge and practical application (praxis), mediated through reflection in and on practice, ECTs made advances in relation to self-efficacy, knowledge and understanding in one year (Ovenden-Hope et al., 2018). This example suggests the importance of building reflective practice into professional development opportunities for ECTs. When teachers engage in structured reflection that connects theory to practice and encourages them to evaluate the impact of their teaching decisions, they developed not only technical skills, but also the professional judgement that characterises effective teaching.

Effective professional development therefore is integral to supporting ECTs and enhancing their long-term career prospects. However, not all professional development is created equal. There are several key features that have been evidenced to support effective professional development (Darling-Hammond et al., 2017), which are:

1. content focus;
2. active learning;
3. collaboration;
4. use of models and modelling;
5. coaching and expert mentor support;
6. feedback and reflection;
7. sustained duration.

As a school leader, ensuring that your professional development offer aligns with these features can significantly impact the effectiveness of your support for ECTs. To support their retention, clear career progression pathways are essential for retaining ambitious teachers (Sims, 2020). Teachers who are aware of opportunities for career advancement within their schools, and how to achieve career progression across the profession, are more likely to remain in teaching (Sims, 2020; Ovenden-Hope et al., 2020). Developing and communicating career pathways should considered for any teacher retention strategy.

SCHOOL CULTURE

The culture you foster as a school leader significantly influences ECTs' experiences, development and decisions about remaining in the profession. A supportive school culture can buffer the challenges inherent in early career teaching and provide the conditions necessary for professional growth and job satisfaction. Collegial relationships and collaborative working environments are crucial for teacher retention (Simon and Johnson, 2015). ECTs particularly benefit from schools where collaboration is normalised, questions are welcomed, risks are encouraged and mistakes are viewed as learning opportunities. When ECTs feel they belong to a professional community that values their contributions while supporting their development, they are more likely to invest in their careers. As a school leader, you have the power to shape a school culture that supports and values ECTs. This includes:

1. creating a welcoming, inclusive and *safe to be vulnerable* environment;
2. fostering collaborative relationships among staff;
3. providing consistent and constructive feedback, support and appropriate challenge;
4. recognising and celebrating the contributions of ECTs;
5. modelling a commitment to continuous learning and improvement.

You will also need to explicitly acknowledge that teaching is complex and challenging, especially in the early years. By treating the challenges of early career teaching as normal, you can reduce the isolation and self-doubt that many ECTs experience. Creating supportive values, such as protecting ECTs from the most challenging groups to teach, or ensuring their workload is manageable, will establish a supportive school culture that complements other strategies to enhance ECT retention and progression.

The second part of this chapter focuses on practical strategies for school leaders to support ECT retention and development. These approaches build on the theoretical foundations established earlier and offer concrete actions you can take to create an environment where ECTs thrive. It is important to remember that these strategies should be adapted for your specific school context.

PRACTICAL STRATEGIES FOR SCHOOL LEADERS

As a school leader, you play a crucial role in establishing systems that support ECT induction and development beyond the minimum requirements of the ECF.

CREATING SYSTEMS THAT SUPPORT ECT DEVELOPMENT

While the ECF provides a clear structure for compliance, your leadership can enhance its implementation to create a truly supportive experience in several key ways.

- *Consider how to implement effective mentoring programmes.* The quality of mentoring significantly influences ECT development (Ovenden-Hope and Kirkpatrick, 2024), yet simply assigning mentors without adequate preparation and support may yield limited benefits (Hobson et al., 2009). Invest in training for mentors that goes beyond the basics of the ECF to develop skills in fostering reflective dialogue, providing constructive feedback and supporting autonomous professional growth. Create clear expectations and protected time for mentoring conversations, ensuring that these focus not just on immediate classroom challenges, but also on deeper pedagogical thinking and career development.

- *Design structured reflective practice opportunities that become embedded in school culture.* You can enhance this by creating regular reflection points in the school calendar, providing templates or prompts that guide meaningful reflection and modelling reflective practice in your own leadership. Consider implementing learning journals, video reflection protocols, or structured peer observation cycles that normalise reflection as an ongoing professional habit (Sellars, 2017).
- *Consider combining development approaches,* such as coaching alongside mentoring, action learning sets and professional learning communities, as multifaceted approaches to ECT development have been found to be most effective in addressing different aspects of professional growth by enhancing ECT self-efficacy, confidence and quality of teaching in differing but complementary ways (Ovenden-Hope et al., 2018).

DEVELOPING A GROWTH-ORIENTED SCHOOL CULTURE

Creating a school culture that actively fosters growth and values ECTs' contributions represents perhaps your most powerful lever for improving retention. Several approaches deserve consideration.

- *Adopt leadership approaches that explicitly foster self-efficacy.* This includes creating opportunities for early success, celebrating growth and impact and providing specific, professional growth-focused feedback (Goddard et al., 2017). When giving feedback to ECTs, highlight concrete examples of their positive impact on students, helping them to see the connection between their actions and student outcomes. This builds the belief that they can make a difference – the essence of self-efficacy.
- *Prioritise creating time and space for professional development.* In the busy life of schools, professional learning can easily become marginalised. Demonstrate your commitment to ECT development by protecting time for it in the school timetable and calendar. Consider implementing models like instructional rounds, lesson study, or professional learning communities that embed development in the routine work of teaching rather than treating it as an add-on (Sims and Fletcher-Wood, 2021).
- *Find meaningful ways to recognise and value ECT contributions.* ECTs bring fresh perspectives, recent training and often unique skills to your school. Create forums where their voices can be heard and their ideas considered. This might include inviting ECTs to contribute to curriculum development, participate in working groups, or share insights

from their initial teacher education. Feeling professionally valued significantly impacts retention (Kelchtermans, 2017).

- *The culture you create should explicitly value learning at all career stages.* When ECTs see more experienced colleagues, including school leaders, engaged in their own learning, this normalises professional growth as an ongoing process rather than a deficit to be addressed in new teachers. Consider how your own learning is visible to staff and how you model engagement with research and reflective practice (Leithwood et al., 2020).

BALANCING SUPPORT AND AUTONOMY

A critical consideration for school leaders is finding the right balance between support and autonomy for ECTs. While structured support is essential, excessive prescription can undermine the development of professional judgement and self-efficacy. Try to create what might be called *structured autonomy* – clear frameworks and expectations coupled with meaningful opportunities for ECTs to make professional decisions and see their impact.

The ECF materials acknowledge this balance when discussing reflective practice, as noted above. This suggests a process where ECTs are active agents in their own development, making decisions and evaluating their impact, rather than simply following prescriptions. As a school leader, you can support this balance by establishing systems and structures that:

1. establish clear expectations and frameworks while encouraging professional judgement within them;
2. provide opportunities for regular, specific feedback that helps ECTs evaluate their impact;
3. create opportunities for ECTs to make meaningful decisions about their teaching;
4. gradually increase ECT autonomy in practice as confidence and competence develop;
5. recognise and celebrate instances where ECTs demonstrate initiative and professional judgement.

This approach will help ECTs develop the decision-making skills that characterise effective teaching while ensuring they have the support needed to succeed. It also communicates trust in their professional capabilities, enhancing their sense of value within the school community (Ryan and Deci, 2020).

ENGAGING WITH RESEARCH AND EVIDENCE

The ECF emphasises the importance of learning from educational research as part of reflective practice. As a school leader, you can enhance ECT development by creating structures that support engagement with research and evidence. The RETAIN programme referenced above provided ECTs with research handbooks that included 'summaries of core research findings, to enable the ECTs to understand, reflect on and apply evidence in their teaching choices' (Ovenden-Hope et al., 2018, p. 5). This model recognised that research engagement is most effective when it is curated and connected explicitly to practice decisions.

You might consider:

1. creating a school research library with accessible summaries of key findings from education research;
2. establishing journal clubs or research discussion groups where ECTs can explore evidence with colleagues;
3. modelling research engagement in your own leadership decisions;
4. connecting with local universities, or the nearest research school network, to co-create research opportunities;
5. encouraging small-scale action research projects that enable ECTs (and all teachers) to investigate aspects of their own practice.

When ECTs engage with research, they develop a deeper understanding of the principles underlying effective practice, enhancing their ability to make informed decisions across different contexts. This contributes to both their effectiveness and their sense of professional identity, supporting long-term retention (Brown and Greany, 2018).

IMPLEMENTATION CHALLENGES AND SOLUTIONS

Implementing effective ECT support faces several common challenges, but anticipating these allows you to develop proactive solutions. Resource constraints present perhaps the most immediate challenge. Quality mentoring, professional development and reflective opportunities all require time, which means funding. Rather than treating ECT development as an add-on to existing structures, look for opportunities to integrate support into the fabric of school operations. This might include rethinking meeting structures to incorporate professional learning, creating efficient documentation processes for reflection, or identifying non-teaching staff who can support aspects of the ECF implementation (Kraft and Papay, 2014).

Financial constraints may also limit what seems possible. Here, consider collaborative approaches with other schools to share resources, costs and expertise. Networks of schools can jointly fund specialist input, create shared professional development opportunities, or establish cross-school mentoring relationships that bring fresh perspectives. The evidence suggests that closing local pay gaps between teaching and non-teaching jobs is key to improving teacher supply – reducing the pay gap by 10 per cent in the worst-affected regions could result in significant increases in teacher numbers (Fullard and Zuccollo, 2021). While individual school leaders may have limited influence over national pay scales, you might consider creative approaches to non-financial benefits that enhance the overall value proposition of teaching in your school.

Another significant challenge is maintaining momentum beyond the formal ECF requirements. The two-year framework provides a foundation, but teacher development continues well beyond this period. Consider how your school's professional development pathway extends the ECT entitlement into years three, four and five of their career – the period when many teachers leave the profession. This might include graduated leadership opportunities, ongoing mentoring relationships (perhaps with the ECT transitioning to mentoring others), or specialised development pathways aligned with career aspirations (Ronfeldt and McQueen, 2017).

Measuring impact represents a final key challenge. How do you know if your approaches to supporting ECTs are working? Develop a multifaceted evaluation approach that includes both quantitative measures (retention rates, progression to leadership roles) and qualitative indicators (job satisfaction, sense of self-efficacy, confidence). Regular surveys, focus groups and structured conversations with ECTs can provide valuable feedback for refining your approach. Remember that the ultimate measure of success is not just whether teachers stay in your school, but whether they thrive and develop as professionals (Sims and Fletcher-Wood, 2021).

CONCLUSION

Supporting ECT retention and development represents one of the most significant leadership challenges and opportunities in education today. Through understanding the factors that influence teacher retention, particularly self-efficacy, reflective practice and meaningful professional development, you can create school environments where new teachers not only stay, but also flourish professionally. The ECF provides a foundation, but your leadership can enhance and extend its impact through thoughtful implementation and complementary initiatives. By creating systems and structures that support development, fostering a growth-oriented culture and proactively addressing implementation challenges you can significantly improve ECT experiences and outcomes in your school.

Remember that teacher retention is not simply about keeping people in posts; it's about developing a profession where individuals can grow, contribute meaningfully and find satisfaction throughout their careers. By investing in ECTs today, you build not only the staff team you need now, but also the profession's leadership for tomorrow.

As you reflect on your own approach to supporting ECTs, consider these questions:

1. how does your school culture actively value and utilise the contributions of ECTs?
2. what systems do you have in place to develop self-efficacy in your ECTs?
3. how do you balance structured support with meaningful autonomy?

4. what opportunities exist for ECTs to engage in reflective practice that genuinely informs their teaching?
5. how do you extend development beyond the formal ECF requirements?

By addressing these questions through evidence-informed approaches, you can create a school environment that not only attracts, but also retains and develops the teachers that our education system so desperately needs.

FURTHER LEARNING

- National Foundation for Education Research (NFER) (2025) *Teacher Labour Market in England Annual Report*. Available at: www.nfer.ac.uk/publications/teacher-labour-market-in-england-annual-report-2025/ (accessed 4 August 2025).

  Since 2018 the NFER has issued an annual report that monitors the progress the education system in England is making towards meeting the teacher supply challenge by measuring the key indicators of teacher supply and working conditions. The most current report will ensure you understand the context of recruitment and retention for your school in relation to the teaching workforce as a whole.

- Ovenden-Hope, Blandford, Cain and Maxwell (2018) RETAIN early career teacher retention programme: evaluating the role of research informed continuing professional development for a high-quality, sustainable 21st century teaching profession *Journal of Education for Teaching* 44(5): 590–607.

  This research offers valuable insights into a successful model for supporting ECTs, with particular relevance for schools in areas of socio-economic disadvantage. The programme's focus on building reflective practice, in-school expertise and professional learning communities provides a practical template for school leaders looking to enhance their ECT support systems.

- Ovenden-Hope and Kirkpatrick (2025) *Early Career Teacher Entitlement: Great Expectations*. London: Hachette Learning.

  This book explores the policies and reforms informing ECT development and the intention of these reforms to improve teacher retention. It examines concepts of quality in teaching and how to implement effective professional development. The book uses the voices of 50 teachers to explore how the ECF was experienced by ECTs, mentors and induction tutors and uses the findings to make recommendations on ECT entitlement in the future.

REFERENCES

Allen, B., Ford, I. and Hannay, T. (2023) *Teacher Recruitment and Retention in 2023*. London: TeacherTapp, Gatsby, SchoolDash.

Allen, R. and Sims, S. (2018) Do pupils from low-income families get low-quality teachers? Indirect evidence from English schools. *Oxford Review of Education*, 44(4), 441–58.

Bandura, A. (2012) On the functional properties of perceived self-efficacy revisited. *Journal of Management*, 38(1), 9–44. https://doi.org/10.1177/0149206311410606

Booth, S. (2024) Teaching workforce grows by just 259 as recruitment stalls. 6 June. Available at: https://schoolsweek.co.uk/teaching-workforce-grows-by-just-259-as-recruitment-stalls/ (accessed: 1 May 2025).

Brown, C. and Greany, T. (2018) The evidence-informed school system in England: where should school leaders be focusing their efforts? *Leadership and Policy in Schools*, 17(1), 115–37. https://doi.org/10.1080/15700763.2016.1270330

Cordingley, P., Crisp, B., Johns, P., Perry, T., Campbell, C. and Bradbury, M. (2019) *Constructing Teachers' Professional Identities*. Brussels: Education International Research.

Darling-Hammond, L., Hyler, M.E. and Gardner, M. (2017) *Effective Teacher Professional Development*. London: Learning Policy Institute.

Department for Education (DfE) (2019a) *Teacher Recruitment and Retention Strategy*. Available at: https://assets.publishing.service.gov.uk/media/5c8fc653ed915d07a80a33fa/DFE_Teacher_Retention_Strategy_Report.pdf (accessed: 1 May 2025).

DfE (2019b) *Early Career Framework*. Available at: https://assets.publishing.service.gov.uk/media/60795936d3bf7f400b462d74/Early-Career_Framework_April_2021.pdf (accessed: 1 May 2025).

DfE (2024a) *Initial Teacher Training and Early Career Framework*. Available at: https://assets.publishing.service.gov.uk/media/65b8fa60e9e10a00130310b2/Initial_teacher_training_and_early_career_framework_30_Jan_2024.pdf (accessed 5 April 2024).

DfE (2024b) *School Workforce in England*. Available at: https://explore-education-statistics.service.gov.uk/find-statistics/school-workforce-in-england#dataBlock-a47f5dc9-567f-4385-8bff-7e01e249884e-charts (accessed: 1 May 2025).

DfE (2024c) *Outcomes of the Review of the Initial Teacher Training Core Content Framework and Early Career Framework*. Available at: https://assets.publishing.service.gov.uk/media/661d24ba08c3be25cfbd3e62/Outcomes_of_the_review_of_the_Initial_Teacher_Training_Core_Content_Framework_and_Early_Career_Framework.pdf (accessed 1 May 2025).

Farrell, T.S. (2016) *Promoting Teacher Reflection in Second Language Education: A Framework for TESOL Professionals*. Oxford: Routledge.

Finlay, L. (2006) *Reflecting on 'Reflective Practice'*. Available at: https://oro.open.ac.uk/68945/1/Finlay-%282008%29-Reflecting-on-reflective-practice-PBPL-paper-52.pdf (accessed: 1 May 2025).

Fullard, J. and Zuccollo, J. (2021) *Local Pay and Teacher Retention in England*. London: Education Policy Institute.

Goddard, R., Goddard, Y., Kim, E.S. and Miller, R. (2017) A theoretical and empirical analysis of the roles of instructional leadership, teacher collaboration, and collective efficacy beliefs in support of student learning. *American Journal of Education*, 121.

Harland, J., Bradley, E. and Worth, J. (2023) *Understanding the Factors that Support the Recruitment and Retention of Teachers: Review of Flexible Working Approaches*. London: Education Endowment Foundation.

Hobson, A.J., Ashby, P., Malderez, A. and Tomlinson, P. (2009) Mentoring beginning teachers: what we know and what we don't. *Teaching and Teacher Education*, 25(1), 207–16.

Howson, J. (2020) Shortages, what shortages? Exploring school workforce supply in England. In T. Ovenden-Hope and R. Passy (eds), *Exploring Teacher Recruitment and Retention: Contextual Challenges from International Perspectives*. Oxford: Routledge, pp. 9–21.

Kelchtermans, G. (2017) 'Should I stay or should I go?': Unpacking teacher attrition/retention as an educational issue. *Teachers and Teaching*, 23(8), 961–77. https://doi.org/10.1080/13540602.2017.1379793

Klassen, R.M. and Chiu, M.M. (2011) The occupational commitment and intention to quit of practicing and pre-service teachers: influence of self-efficacy, job stress, and teaching context. *Contemporary Educational Psychology*, 36(2), 114–29.

Klassen, R.M. and Tze, V.M. (2014) Teachers' self-efficacy, personality, and teaching effectiveness: a meta-analysis. *Educational Research Review*, 12, 59–76. https://doi.org/10.1016/j.edurev.2014.06.001

Kraft, M.A. and Papay, J.P. (2014) Can professional environments in schools promote teacher development? Explaining heterogeneity in returns to teaching experience. *Educational Evaluation and Policy Analysis*, 36(4), 476–500. https://doi.org/10.3102/0162

Leithwood, K., Harris, A. and Hopkins, D. (2020) Seven strong claims about successful school leadership revisited. *School Leadership and Management*, 40(1), 5–22. https://doi.org/10.1080/13632434.2019.1596077

McClean, D., Worth, J. and Smith, A. (2024) *Teacher Labour Marking in England. Annual Report 2024*. Slough: NFER. Available at: www.nfer.ac.uk/media/hqdglvra/teacher_labour_market_in_england_annual_report_2024.pdf (accessed 2 May 2025).

Ovenden-Hope, T. (2023) The great supply crisis: can the Early Career Framework appease early career teacher recruitment and retention challenges in England? *Impact*, 17, Chartered College of Teaching.

Ovenden-Hope, T. and Kirkpatrick, H. (2024) The Early Career Framework: why context matters for teacher professional development. *Education Sciences*, 14, 1261. https://doi.org/10.3390/educsci14111261

Ovenden-Hope, T. and Kirkpatrick, H. (2025) *Early Career Teacher Entitlement: Great Expectations*. London: John Catt/Hachette.

Ovenden-Hope, T., Blandford, S., Cain, T. and Maxwell, B. (2018) RETAIN early career teacher retention programme: Evaluating the role of research informed continuing professional development for a high-quality, sustainable 21st century teaching profession. *Journal of Education for Teaching*, 44(5), 590-607. https://doi.org/10.1080/02607476.2018.1516349.

Ovenden-Hope, T., Blandford, S., Cain, T. and Maxwell, B. (2020) RETAIN: a research-informed model of continuing professional development for early career teacher retention.

In T. Ovenden-Hope and R. Passy (eds), *Exploring Recruitment and Retention: Contextual Challenges from International Perspectives*. Oxford: Routledge, pp. 59–72.

Ovenden-Hope, T., Passy, R. and Iglehart, P. (2022) Educational isolation and the challenge of 'place' for securing a high-quality teacher supply. In I. Mentor, *The Palgrave Handbook Teacher Education Research*. London: Palgrave Macmillan, pp. 1–22.

Pollard, E., Williams, C., Nancarrow, A., Talbot, J., Cook, J., Williams, J., Bajorek, Z. and Illidge, L. (2024) *Teachers' Professional Development Journeys: A Report for Ofsted*. London: Institute of Employment Studies.

Ronfeldt, M. and McQueen, K. (2017) Does new teacher induction really improve retention? *Journal of Teacher Education*, 68(4), 394–410. https://doi.org/10.1177/0022487117702583

Ryan, R.M. and Deci, E.L. (2020) Intrinsic and extrinsic motivation from a self-determination theory perspective: definitions, theory, practices, and future directions. *Contemporary Educational Psychology*, 61, 101860. https://doi.org/10.1016/j.cedpsych

Schön, D.A. (1983) *The Reflective Practitioner: How Professionals Think in Action*. London: Basic Books.

Sellars, M. (2017) *Reflective Practice for Teachers* (2nd ed.). London: Sage.

Sibieta, L. (2020) *Teacher Shortages in England: Analysis and Pay Options*. London: Education Policy Institute.

Simon, N.S. and Johnson, S.M. (2015) Teacher turnover in high-poverty schools: what we know and can do. *Teachers College Record*, 117(3), 1–36.

Sims, S. (2020) Modelling the relationships between teacher working conditions, job satisfaction and workplace mobility. *British Educational Research Journal*, 46(2), 301–20.

Sims, S. and Fletcher-Wood, H. (2021) Identifying the characteristics of effective teacher professional development: a critical review. *School Effectiveness and School Improvement*, 32(1), 47–63. https://doi.org/10.1080/09243453.2020.1772841

Tschannen-Moran, M. and Hoy, A.W. (2001) Teacher efficacy: capturing an elusive construct. *Teaching and Teacher Education*, 17(7), 783–805. https://doi.org/10.1016/S0742-051X(01)00036-1

Veenman, S. (1984) Perceived problems of beginning teachers. *Review of Educational Research*, 54(2), 143–78.

Walker, M., Worth, J., Liht, J., Classick, R., Tang, S. and Straw, S. (2024) *Evaluation of the Early Roll-out of the Early Career Framework*. London: Education Endowment Foundation.

Woolfolk Hoy, A. and Burke Spero, R. (2005) Changes in teacher efficacy during the early years of teaching: a comparison of four measures. *Teaching and Teacher Education*, 21(4), 343–56.

Worth, J. and Van den Brande, J. (2020) *Teacher Autonomy: How Does It Relate*. Slough: NFER.

Zee, M. and Koomen, H.M. (2016) Teacher self-efficacy and its effects on classroom processes, student academic adjustment, and teacher well-being: a synthesis of 40 years of research. *Review of Educational Research*, 86(4), 981–1015. https://doi.org/10.31

9
FLEXIBLE WORKING PRACTICES TO SUPPORT RECRUITMENT, RETENTION AND CAREER DEVELOPMENT

LUCY ROSE AND LINDSAY PATIENCE

INTRODUCTION

Staff are both your greatest asset and your greatest expense. They make the difference between good and great outcomes for their students (Sutton Trust, 2011), so keeping them in your school or in our profession more generally is a key responsibility for leaders in education. Recruitment and retention are big stressors locally and nationally. Budgeting and resources are scarce and finite. The challenge is that schools are client-facing, human environments where small in-person interactions can make a huge difference to those we serve. So why would we consider flexibility in our sector at all? This chapter explores why we must consider flexible working – in spite of our initial perceived barriers – as a powerful tool to recruit and, most importantly, retain brilliant educators who will ensure the best outcomes for the children in our schools.

In this chapter, we share:

- the key benefits of exploring flexible working;
- the reason flexible working is a priority now;

- the changing flexible working landscape;
- how flexible working might look in a setting like yours.

BEGIN WITH THE WHY

What began with anecdotal stories of teachers and leaders having 'no choice' but to leave the profession, then sharing these and hearing more, similar stories was a powerful driver in the initial stages of our work in this area. Our inbox was dominated by messages with a familiar pattern of despair, guilt and frustration with a system which did not have the capacity to adapt to changing circumstances. Reassuringly, these individual stories are backed up with robust data proving much of what we suspected: flexible working implemented thoughtfully and proactively can have a positive impact on pupil outcomes.

The data (for example, Cooper Gibson, 2019; NFER's *Teacher Labour Market Annual Report 2015* and subsequent reports) shows us that flexible working is beneficial in four key ways. Flexible working supports:

- teacher recruitment and retention;
- staff wellbeing;
- diversity, equity, inclusion and belonging (DEIB).

HOW DOES FLEXIBLE WORKING SUPPORT RETENTION AND WELLBEING?

In almost all of our consultations with leaders about their resistance to flexibility, the response falls into one of two camps: logistical impossibility or fear of the 'floodgates opening'. Yet, where headteachers have embraced elements of flexible working in their setting and consulted with staff, they are pleasantly surprised by how little staff demand and how easy their requests are to accommodate. Far from being a logistical nightmare, having flexible options at the heart of the timetabling process helps to create a culture of trust which is welcomed and valued by its employees. Elements of flexibility in a role often negate the preoccupation with presenteeism and demonstrate to employees that they are entrusted to complete the necessary work without being watched. Essentially, being allowed to choose when, where and how we complete elements of our role helps us to feel trusted. With trust comes empowerment, loyalty and productivity. Demonstrating that we trust our staff helps retain them. We want our schools to be high-trust organisations and embedding elements of flexibility is one way to demonstrate this.

An organisation which is comfortable allowing their employees to work flexibly demonstrates a mature attitude to other key skills like communication. Meetings are not taken up with admin as this is shared in a weekly, printed bulletin. Key information is readily available and communicated effectively whether a member of staff is present or not. For more information on the neuroscience behind building trustworthiness and raising levels of oxytocin at work, take a look at the work of neuroscientist Paul J Zak, Professor of Economic Sciences, Psychology and Management at Oregon University; he shares evidence of the benefits, such as colleagues feeling more satisfied and happier with life both in and outside work (Zak et al., 2005).

The two largest groups leaving teaching are retirees and women aged 30–9. Teaching is a physically demanding job and this does not relent as we get older. The institutional and pedagogical knowledge held by our oldest and most experienced colleagues is cherished and their knowledge of nurturing young people is vital. It is detrimental to our sector to lose this precious wisdom early because we are not willing to entertain the value of flexible options. Our inbox shares examples of colleagues who feel forced to leave the profession before they are ready simply because the prospect of a full week is too much. There are additional elements which complicate this for those whose pension will be relative to their final salary (rather than their career average), but leaving before you're ready and taking all that institutional knowledge with you is a loss keenly felt. Discussions with those close to retirement about how to support them, such as with staggered or compressed hours, can create smooth succession planning, minimising disruption for students and helping to alleviate the premature drain of our treasured colleagues from the sector.

Our second biggest group, women aged 30–9, has jumped from 6,000 when we began this work in 2016 to over 9,000 in the 2023–4 academic year. Thankfully, under the leadership of Emma Sheppard, the MTPT Project's support of parent teachers and tireless pressure for adequate research produced *The Missing Mothers Report* (McShane and Sheppard, 2024) in collaboration with the New Britain Project. This report pays attention to this demographic and makes nine recommendations which we would be unwise to ignore, including a commitment at national level to share best flexible working practices which will support our colleagues. Our inbox is overwhelmingly dedicated to supporting those who request flexible working as carers – for young children, for ageing parents or 'sandwich caring' for both. Failing to plan support for our predominantly female staff at the point in their lives when the majority of care falls to them is pushing them out of the profession. Evidence suggests that they do not leave altogether, but step down and/or take roles which are in the education sector, but allow greater flexibility: in policy, admin or as teaching and learning assistants (TLAs) (Worth et al., 2015). This and subsequent reports note teachers of this demographic in new, reduced-capacity posts five years later: it was flexibility they were seeking (NFER, 2015).

Poor communication and the protracted anxiety during parental leave of the potential outcome of a flexible working request are the most commonly cited examples we receive for why we lose another swathe of employees. While this valuable focus embeds at a national level, we must look to our responsibilities at our own institutions: what are we doing to ensure that we retain our female middle and senior leaders at this stage in their lives? On average two to three per year will need our support in our contexts. Note too that many more will be watching how this is handled and then making a decision about whether this organisation (or this profession) is viable with plans for a family or whether to 'leave before they leave' and jump ship to a new profession before entering that phase in their lives. The MTPT Project (www.mtpt.org.uk) offers training for line managers and coaching for those with parental responsibilities across all regions of England and many of these opportunities are sponsored or subsidised. The coaching model can be offered to returners as part of their Keeping in Touch (KIT) days and proves to be successful in retaining teachers and leaders at this often-vulnerable transition in their lives. Supporting our colleagues to manage two highly immersive roles of teaching and parenthood is incredibly empowering and ought to be standard practice if we are serious about retention.

Beyond these two significant groups, in 2019, three quarters (76 per cent) of surveyed teachers reported that they would be more likely to remain in the profession long term if they could work flexibly (Cooper Gibson, 2019). We remember that this was pre-pandemic, when flexible working practices were not so widely publicised and when schools had rarely entertained the online options already commonplace in other sectors such as online meetings and remote working. It is fair to say that much of what had previously been considered 'impossible' in education was reversed overnight as schools had no choice but to meet remotely and communicate efficiently. While there are few teachers who would return to wholesale online learning, the elements of flexibility explored and enjoyed during that time have generated discussion in settings where it was previously considered an unlikely possibility. Providing a window into the lives and priorities of colleagues opened the eyes of leaders to the whole teacher and meant that more interest was taken into how to harness and nurture those parts of their lives for the benefit of them as individuals and to the whole school community. Educators too saw into the lives of those in other sectors and, liking the flexible elements of what they saw, moved into sectors which afforded greater flexibility. It is no surprise then that by 2021, 82 per cent (IFF, 2021) of leaders surveyed who offered flexible working agreed that it had helped to retain teachers and leaders who might otherwise have left. The more proactive we can be about providing elements of flexibility which produce the most value for the individual while bolstering the values of the organisation, the better. The demand is there and, for the sake of the learners in our care, we must find ways to meet it.

HOW DOES FLEXIBLE WORKING SUPPORT RECRUITMENT?

In our experience of working with schools, school leaders often face difficulties in recruiting teachers and leaders. Staffing the school is crucial to its smooth and effective operation and failing to appoint staff can have serious implications both financially and in terms of the quality of teaching and learning and leadership. Having effective teachers in the classroom is critical and this is even more important for our most vulnerable groups of students.

In situations where class teachers cannot be appointed, we often hear that schools turn to supply agencies, which can be costly. As well as potentially being relatively expensive, there can also be difficulties with settling in, building relationships and quality of pedagogy. Anecdotally, we hear that where there are gaps in leadership positions, more responsibility and pressure is added to the workload of others. In a profession where workload is already seen as high, unfilled vacancies may be making the situation even worse.

So how can flexible working help? Advertising posts with flexibility can actually increase the application conversion rate on applications by up to 19 per cent according to TES data (TESGlobalCorp, 2017), although it should be noted that advertising posts with flexibility did not increase conversion rates across all subjects (e.g. it decreased conversion rates in PE by up to 8 per cent). For some subjects it could increase the chances of being able to recruit successfully, which is beneficial particularly in certain secondary subjects where there may be a shortage of applicants. For sciences, advertising flexibly can increase your chances of success by 13 per cent. Stating a commitment to flexibility, even for full-time posts, can make the role and school more attractive to potential candidates. With the change in law effective from July 2024, candidates may request a level of flexibility from day 1, so being prepared for these conversations will pay dividends. Among schools that offer flexible working, 53 per cent of surveyed leaders said that flexible working helped to attract a greater number of candidates (IFF, 2021).

Changing working practices post-pandemic across other sectors has meant that competitor careers have scope for offering lots of flexibility. This could have a considerable impact on the ability of schools to recruit and retain staff if they cannot offer any flexibility at all. It is clear that schools cannot have all teachers working from home like other sectors do, but it does make it more imperative that we offer some flexible options which are best suited to our context. Options include:

- remote working (PPA offsite);
- staggered hours;
- compressed hours;
- annualised hours;
- time off in lieu;
- talent partnerships (job share);
- part-time.

We do need to make teaching a viable, sustainable and attractive career. We need to be able to market the profession in a competitive way. For 2021–2, the highest out-of-service leaving rate in England's schools was for under 25s, with 11.9 per cent leaving in 2021–2 (DfE, 2022). Is it possible that a level of flexibility at the start of their career might help mitigate against the overwhelm that new teachers feel and ensure that they remain in the profession? Conversations we have with younger teachers now demonstrate a genuine understanding of boundaries and wellbeing. They do not shy away from the workload or the responsibilities of teaching, but can see that continuing at a particular pace when they are still learning their craft is likely to lead to burnout. They want to have a lifelong career in teaching and yet they can predict that it will not be sustainable. In the past five years, our inbox has included so many more requests for flexibility from younger teachers with precisely this outlook.

The way our younger generation view work has changed. With lifelong experience of agile study and tech-based learning, it makes sense that 92 per cent of 18–34-year-olds (Timewise, 2017) use or want an element of flexible working in their future profession regardless of the sector they wanted to work in. A future workforce which anticipates flexibility is at risk of discounting education entirely if flexibility is not commonplace.

It is not just young or new teachers who want flexibility. Now Teach is a training and development scheme for career changers who want to become teachers. Now Teach reports that many of their trainees want to work flexibly once they are trained. These particular teachers come from outside the education sector so their experience in the world of work outside the institution of school means that they bring fresh insights which can be beneficial.

Key findings from the most recent *Working Lives of Teachers and Leaders* report (McLean et al., 2023), also highlighted that teachers' ability to work from home, a key flexible working arrangement and feature of post-pandemic working life, remains very limited. This may constitute a further competitive threat while the prevalence of home working in the workforce outside teaching remains high. Given the findings of this most recent NFER report, you should feel supported in exploring options which will work in your context as an absolute priority if staffing is going to be tackled at local and national level.

HOW DOES FLEXIBLE WORKING SUPPORT DIVERSITY, EQUITY, INCLUSION AND BELONGING?

Our schools are often the first community which our children are part of and curate the messaging they receive implicitly about how communities are run. A profession which attracts predominantly white, cis, female, able-bodied employees cannot help but develop bias in the children we serve. There is wonderful work to address this through powerful grassroots initiatives looking to diversify the demographic of teachers: BAMEEd; DiverseEd; Men Teach Primary; Black Men Teach. Organisations which share the adage that 'you cannot be what you cannot see' seek to encourage under-represented groups into the profession and we welcome their important work. So what has this got to do with flexibility? Two key areas where flexibility and diversity, equity, inclusion and belonging (DEIB) intersect are the gender pay gap and the inclusion of those with physical disabilities (congenital or acquired) in the profession.

The education sector has one of the widest gender pay gaps (ASCL, 2016). For a sector which employs predominantly female teachers, this is a situation which must be addressed. For the past four years, the MTPT Project and WomenEd have hosted an annual online event 'The Mother of All Pay Gaps' to draw attention to the issues and updates relevant to our sector. This is in part due to lack of flexibility and to the current wording of the school teachers' pay and conditions (STPCD) surrounding teaching and learning responsibility (TLR) payments which states that TLRs must match any pro rata arrangement. In other words, if a middle leader requests a reduction in hours, their TLR should also be reduced. If I was a head of subject on a TLR shifting temporarily from full time to 0.6 while my children are in nursery, I would need to accept the reduction of my TLR payment in addition to losing 40 per cent of my salary. Consider that in the reality of a school. Unless negotiations have been made with other colleagues in the department to take on elements of the head of subject role, I will still be expected to fulfil the role in less time and for less money. For the individual, it makes little sense financially or practically – so they inevitably step down. We have been campaigning tirelessly for the wording to be changed, and we hope that the eventual edit will empower school leaders to address this pay gap.

The second area in which we have anecdotal evidence that flexibility would have a positive impact on DIEB is in allowing less able-bodied colleagues and those suffering with chronic illness to remain part of the profession. Reasonable adjustments must be made in law as part of the Equalities Act and individual circumstances are unique. However, being a profession open to a level of flexibility for all can, for example, allow for appointments at times when pain must be alleviated more regularly; when later starts would allow for a more energised day; where reduced hours would be welcomed and not considered an administrative burden before a colleague even steps through the door.

Our book, *Flex Education: A Guide for Flexible Working in Schools* (Patience and Rose, 2022), goes into much more detail about each of these areas and there is now a wealth of information as part of a suite of webinars created for the DfE to support schools on their flexible journey.

WHY NOW?

Flexible working in schools isn't always seen as easy or possible to do, but the DfE is committed to supporting schools in overcoming the challenges associated with flexible working because of the many benefits associated with flexible working. It is a key priority set out in the Recruitment and Retention Strategy (DfE, 2019) and the commitment to promoting and expanding access to flexible working for all teachers and leaders was also reinforced in the Staff Wellbeing Charter (DfE, 2021), which includes flexible working as a key pillar.

The education sector is behind other sectors in terms of flexible working. In a female-dominated sector, 29 per cent of female teachers work part time (DfE, 2022) compared to 36 per cent for female employees across all UK sectors (ONS, 2023). People who leave the education sector often go on to work flexibly. NFER analysis of 2020 Annual Survey of Hours and Earnings data found that around a fifth of full-time teachers who left teaching moved into part-time work (Worth and McLean, 2022). Flexible working is gaining momentum across other sectors, so the time for the education sector to start looking at this really is now, especially if we wish to remain a competitive and sustainable career choice.

WHAT DOES IT LOOK LIKE?

Currently, the flexible working landscape in education is a workplace lottery. Although there has been increased uptake and innovation as understanding improves and the evidence becomes more robust, colleagues are still often faced with reactive, outdated models which appear only available for specific groups (parents – mothers) in their setting. This not only can be perceived as 'unfair', but is also objectively unfair due to its feed into the gender pay gap and, if mismanaged, its negative impact on staff agility and skillset. It is worth considering where we sit as a sector and where you sit as an individual on the Timewise Flexible Maturity Scale (2017). When we began this work in 2016, it is fair to say that education was at the very bottom of the curve: tolerating it reluctantly. There were a handful of trailblazers pushing towards open support, but very few actively encouraged flexibility in an education setting. How you feel towards flexible working will be informed by your beliefs about education and examples or non-examples of flexible working you have experienced. Whatever your perception, it is critical to acknowledge it because the 2023 NFER report reveals that the biggest barrier to adoption of flexible working is the opinion of the headteacher (Harland et al., 2023). You have the potential to be part of what one webinar delegate called the quiet revolution: your opinion and the action you take matters.

HOW?

At its best, flexible working is not isolated pockets afforded to a few in exceptional circumstances, but instead part of your organisation's fabric and part of 'the way we do things here'. Whenever we run professional development, the sessions for those requesting flexibility are always much more popular than those supporting the gatekeepers to flexibility. The message is simple: there is more demand than supply. If we are unable to meet that demand, our colleagues will go elsewhere. The case studies which we cite most frequently (Antonia Spinks at the Pioneer Trust; Sue Atkinson at the John Tylor Free School) are where flexibility is at the heart of the people strategy. In both of these overwhelmingly positive case studies, the leaders have looked in detail at their contexts and made decisions about the types of flexibility they can offer there to benefit the students in their care. Table 9.1 shows an ideal shift towards a proactive flexible working people strategy.

Table 9.1 Non-example/example comparison of successful flexible working policy

Non-example	Example
• The school struggles to recruit/retain effective teachers ready for the new academic year	• Remaining posts (or skills from audit) are advertised for and recruited (February–May)
• School manages to partially meet the needs of some flex requests	• School has identified types of flexibility which match its vision and values
• Reactive model where individual requests are responded to ad hoc	• Proactive model incorporated into timetabling process
• Staff who are not in receipt of flexible working arrangements are resentful. Policy exacerbates gender pay gap	• All staff are asked annually whether they will be requesting a flexible option the following year (November)
• Timetabling is managed in isolation: 'ivory tower'; 'who you know' culture; top-down; accountability over skillset	• Timetabling is decided in collaboration with middle leaders and their teams to maximise deployment of effective teachers (December–February)
• Remaining staff feel the impact of low retention. Higher incidence of burnout, long-term sick leave, leave profession altogether	• All staff feel empowered and trusted by a *reason neutral* process which is equitable and supportive

CONCLUSION

Thank you for reading this far and being receptive to our call to action. Thankfully, there now exists a wealth of information available to assist you and your organisation on your flexible journey.

Next steps:

- commit to flexibility within your organisation. Identify a member of the senior leadership team to lead, monitor and evaluate our journey. Signpost them to our FAQ videos or to the wealth of information available on the DfE's Flexible Working in Schools programme website. Use our self-evaluation tool adopted and adapted by the DfE to plot where your organisation is right now;
- encourage them to revisit your school vision to map opportunities for flexibility which align with the values of your organisation. If you need upskilling on types of flexibility, take a look at the webinars and/or read our book – e.g. if pastoral care is a priority at secondary, staggered hours might require a change of tutor time to P2. Where parental contact is critical in primary, talent partnerships (job sharing) might be preferable to staggered hours or PPA offsite;
- consider what you want to improve (staff turnover, staff absence, long-term sick leave, loss of teachers after maternity leave, cost of recruitment …) and audit for monitoring;

- share your process with staff (preliminary; exploratory; work in progress) and involve all colleagues in the conversation by asking them what elements of flexibility they might choose. Although this 'opening the floodgates' can be unnerving, our experience is that headteachers are always pleasantly surprised not only by how little staff ask for, but also how much of a difference it makes;
- commit to implementing elements which suit your specific context and your staff. Trial, monitor, evaluate and refine. Keep communication open. Measure and share your journey. Celebrate success!

Our aim is a national, proactive and supportive system (rather than a patchy and unreliable one), which matches the context and prioritises flexibility suited to your setting, staff and students. Some of this is being tackled at national level, such as revising the STPCD wording and implementing legal changes that ensure teachers can request flexible working arrangements from day one in any role. However, much of the innovation and development of good practice occurs within settings where leaders like you harness flexible working to best support your specific context and the students you serve.

FURTHER LEARNING

- Patience L. and Rose L. (2022) *Flex Education: A Guide for Flexible Working in Schools*. London: Corwin.

  This book explores flexible working in education, combining theoretical perspectives with practical case studies. School leaders can learn how to design and implement flexible working policies that enhance teacher well-being, improve retention and foster innovative school practices.

- Capita (nd) Flexible working support: A programme for Multi-Academy Trusts and Schools. Available at: http://www.flexibleworkingineducation.co.uk (accessed 4 August 2025).

  This website hosts practical guidance, policy templates and real-life examples for implementing flexible working arrangements in schools. School leaders can use these tools to create adaptive work environments that meet the diverse needs of staff while maintaining high standards of educational delivery.

- Sheppard E. (2022) *A Guide to Teaching, Parenting and Creating Family Friendly Schools: The MaternityTeacher PaternityTeacher Project Handbook*. London: Routledge.

  This book examines innovative approaches to flexible working in educational settings, highlighting research findings and case studies from schools that have successfully adopted such practices. School leaders can gain evidence-based insights and actionable strategies to reshape work practices, ultimately supporting teacher retention and enhancing overall school performance.

REFERENCES

ASCL (2016) *Closing the Gender Pay Gap in Education: A Leadership Imperative*. Available at: www.ascl.org.uk/ASCL/media/ASCL/Our%20view/Campaigns/Closing-the-gender-pay-gap-in-Education-a-leadership-imperative.pdf (accessed: 4 May 2025).

Cooper Gibson (2019) *Exploring Flexible Working Practice in Schools*. London: Cooper Gibson Research. Available at: https://assets.publishing.service.gov.uk/media/5fbfb3d4d3bf7f573a80828e/Exploring_flexible_working_practice_in_schools_-_interim_report.pdf (accessed: 4 May 2025).

Department for Education (DfE) (2019) *Teacher Recruitment and Retention Strategy*. Available at: https://assets.publishing.service.gov.uk/media/5c8fc653ed915d07a80a33fa/DFE_Teacher_Retention_Strategy_Report.pdf (accessed: 1 May 2025).

DfE (2021) *Staff Wellbeing Charter*. Available at: www.gov.uk/guidance/education-staff-wellbeing-charter (accessed: 4 May 2025).

DfE (2022) *School Workforce in England*. Available at: https://explore-education-statistics.service.gov.uk/find-statistics/school-workforce-in-england (accessed: 4 May 2025).

Harland J., Bradley E. and Worth J. (2023) *Understanding the factors that support recruitment and retention of teachers - review of flexible working approaches*. Slough: NFER. Available at: https://www.nfer.ac.uk/publications/understanding-the-factors-that-support-the-recruitment-and-retention-of-teachers-review-of-flexible-working-approaches/ (accessed: 27 May 2025).

IFF (2021) *School and College Panel*. London: IFF Research. Available at: https://assets.publishing.service.gov.uk/media/62446733e90e075f15381ccb/SCP_December_Wave_Report_v6.pdf (accessed: 4 May 2025).

McLean D., Worth J. and Faulkner-Ellis H. (2023) *Teacher Labour Market in England: Annual Report 2022*. Slough: NFER.

McShane, A. and Sheppard, E. (2024) *The Missing Mothers Report*. Available at: www.newbritain.org.uk/missing-mothers (accessed: 4 May 2025).

Patience, L. and Rose, L. (2022) *Flex Education: A Guide for Flexible Working in Schools*. London: Corwin.

Office for National Statistics (ONS) (2023) *Gender pay gap in the UK: 2023*. Available at: https://www.ons.gov.uk/employmentandlabourmarket/peopleinwork/earningsandworkinghours/bulletins/genderpaygapintheuk/2023 (accessed: 27 May 2025).

Sheppard, E. (2022) *A Guide to Teaching, Parenting and Creating Family Friendly Schools: The MaternityTeacher PaternityTeacher Project Handbook*. London: Routledge.

TESGlobalCorp (2017) *Flexible Working Recruitment Insights*. London: TES. Available at: www.slideshare.net/TESGlobalCorp/flexible-working-recruitment-insights (accessed: 4 May 2025).

The Sutton Trust (2011) *Improving the impact of teachers on pupil achievement in the UK – interim findings*. Available at: https://www.suttontrust.com/our-research/improving-impact-teachers-pupil-achievement-uk-interim-findings/ (accessed: 27 May 2025).

Timewise (2017) *Flexible Working: A Talent Imperative*. London: Timewise. Available at: https://timewise.co.uk/wp-content/uploads/2019/06/Flexible_working_Talent_Imperative.pdf (accessed: 4 May 2025).

Worth J., Bamford S. and Durban B. (2015) *Should I Stay or Should I Go? NFER Analysis of Teachers Joining and Leaving the Profession*. Slough: NFER. Available at: https://www.nfer.ac.uk/publications/should-i-stay-or-should-i-go-nfer-analysis-of-teachers-joining-and-leaving-the-profession/ (accessed: 27 May 2025).

Worth, J. and Walker, M. (2019) *The Latest Findings From the Teacher Workload Survey 2019*. Slough: NFER. Available at: www.nfer.ac.uk/news-events/nfer-blogs/the-latest-findings-from-the-teacher-workload-survey-2019/ (accessed: 4 May 2025).

Worth J. and McLean D. (2022) *What teachers do next after leaving and its implications for pay-setting*. Slough: NFER.

Zak, P.J., Kurzban, R. and Matzner, W.T. (2005) *Oxytocin is Associated with Human Trustworthiness*. Oregon: NIH.

10

ADDRESSING WORKLOAD AND SUPPORTING TEACHER WELLBEING

YAMINA BIBI

INTRODUCTION

In the teaching profession, challenges around workload and wellbeing do not seem to be diminishing. It is still an area of concern corroborated by the data from teachers and leaders themselves. Government funding may be a key part of the issue facing schools but there are many ways school leaders can support teachers in addressing workload and supporting teacher wellbeing.

School leaders have a duty of care towards every member of the school community and must understand the issues impacting workload in order to ensure staff are able to progress in their careers while maintaining their wellbeing. This chapter explores some of the concerns reported by teachers as impacting their workload and wellbeing and shares some whole-school solutions and suggestions for school leaders to implement.

THE WORKLOAD WORRY

When we look at the data shared about their working lives, serving teachers and those who have left the profession share a concerning picture of teaching as an unsustainable career.

In the *Working Lives of Teachers and Leaders* (WLTL) survey report (DfE, 2024) it was found that primary teachers reported working on average 52.5 hours a week while secondary teachers reported working 50.3 hours a week. The average of 48.1 hours, though a decrease from 49.4 hours the previous year, is still high. When we compare it to other Organisation for Economic Cooperation and Development (OECD) countries, we see how overworked teachers in England really are.

In the book *Support Not Surveillance* (2022), Dr Mary Bousted compared England's results against other OECD countries in the 2018 Teaching and Learning International Survey (TALIS) (Ainley and Carstens, 2018). Bousted found that 'secondary teachers in England reported working an average 49.3 hours a week, against an OECD average of 41 hours' and that 'England is an outlier in its treatment of teachers ... other high-performing nations treat their teachers better and take positive action to develop their potential and protect them from excessive work' (2022, p. 28).

With this data, it is no surprise that in '2022/23, 9.6 per cent of teachers left teaching' by the next year (McLean and Worth, 2025, p. 5). Why are we an outlier in our treatment of teachers in comparison to other countries? What is the excessive work that is driving so many teachers out of a profession they worked hard to enter? If they continue leaving, who will lead our schools in the future?

The perception of teachers about the causes of unacceptable workload offers leaders crucial insights into where we might begin when addressing workload and promoting positive wellbeing.

In the 2024 WLTL survey, 49 per cent of teachers and middle leaders felt their workload was unacceptable, citing administrative tasks (74 per cent), following up on behaviour incidents (60 per cent), parental cooperation and communication (49 per cent), data reporting and analysis (53 per cent) and lesson planning (44 per cent) as key reasons. Though administrative tasks, data reporting and lesson planning have been common concerns over the last few years, the survey found that there was an increase of teachers reporting behaviour, parental cooperation and communication as specific tasks they spent too much of their time on.

When we zoom into concerns about behaviour, interestingly, there is a discrepancy in how leaders view behaviour in their schools and how teachers view behaviour in their schools. While 76 per cent of leaders stated that behaviour was good or very good in their schools, only 45 per cent of teachers stated the same. Is this perhaps because young people may behave differently in the presence of senior leaders due to their role or are senior leaders ignoring the problem because they create the policies which teachers and school staff are expected to implement?

Regardless of this discrepancy between leaders' perception of behaviour in schools and that of teachers, we must acknowledge that 'the drivers of worsening pupil behaviour are complex and multi-faceted, and are likely to be linked in part to pupil mental health and the wider challenges facing the system for supporting pupils with SEND' (McLean and Worth, 2025, p. 8). Complex and multifaceted they may be, particularly after the Covid-19 pandemic, but we cannot shy away from how years of government underfunding of education has directly hindered the ability for schools to provide effective student mental health and wellbeing support.

This is in turn having severe consequences on staff wellbeing and workload. In England, 82 per cent of staff experienced challenging pupil behaviour which directly impacted their mental health and wellbeing negatively. And though teachers suggest that this may be due to unmet emotional, basic and mental needs (Education Support, 2024), we as school leaders must not allow this to inhibit how we challenge disruptive pupil behaviour – particularly when 51 per cent report pupils and students becoming more verbally abusive and 29 per cent feel that they have become more physically abusive.

For those of us who have taught pre- and post- the Covid-19 pandemic, we have experienced first-hand the challenges in student behaviour and the rise of negative behaviour incidents towards teachers and other students. From the data and my own experience, it is clear however, that as adults and professionals, we differ in how we perceive and address this key issue within our schools. With the rise of social media 'edu-influencers' who promote dichotomous views of how we might lead behaviour in schools, you might be led to believe that it is an either/or approach: zero tolerance or a relational approach to behaviour. I believe, like with most aspects of life, that the middle path is perhaps the most effective. A dual approach to behaviour which promotes positive school environments by ensuring young people are supported to regulate their behaviour while being held to account when required is perhaps best.

Interestingly, when interviewing early career teachers (ECTs) as part of the research for my own book, *A Little Guide for Teachers: Thriving in Your First Years of Teaching* (Bibi, 2024), new teachers spoke in depth about the negative impact of deteriorating student behaviour on their wellbeing. Some commented that there was a lack of clarity around their school's behaviour policy and how to apply it consistently which led to them finding managing behaviour in the classroom challenging. One colleague said that they went home most days 'teary, stressed and overwhelmed following behaviour incidents' and were planning to leave following the completion of their second year. A few ECTs I interviewed felt unsupported and undermined by leaders, some of whom would send students back into the classroom despite the teacher requesting for disruptive students to be removed. While establishing behaviour expectations in the classroom is not a new issue for new teachers, the fact that many are leaving as a result of this along with other reasons is recent. McLean and Worth (2025, p. 18) reported (for the National Foundation for Educational Research, NFER) that the school workforce 'data shows that leaving rates for ECTs – teachers in the first two years of their career – are higher than average'. The purpose of the ECF was to support ECTs, but the NFER report suggests that this has had little impact on retention, particularly in the first few years. I think that if we are to ensure that we have schools with teachers in the future, we have to not only address student behaviour, but also how we support ECTs and experienced staff inside and beyond the classroom.

TEACHER WELLBEING

In addition to student behaviour, other aspects of teaching, such as organisational culture, impacts teacher wellbeing. While Ofsted and the high-stakes accountability of exam results can negatively impact school culture, many teachers are aware of these accountability measures existing when they choose to teach. Perhaps what is not always anticipated is the severe stress, exhaustion and anxiety causing some to leave the profession. Is this only as a result of the government funding, Ofsted and school league tables?

Not necessarily. In the *Teacher Wellbeing Index* (Education Support, 2024), shockingly 78 per cent of school staff reported feeling stressed and 79 per cent shared that they had experienced 'physical, psychological or behavioural symptoms due to their work'. As a result, the wellbeing index for staff working in schools was much lower in comparison to the national population. Clearly, schools in England have a significant amount of work to do to increase levels of staff wellbeing if we are to improve staff retention and recruitment.

Of those that reported that their organisation's culture, 50 per cent had a negative effect on their health and wellbeing. When asked to identify what the most important aspects of an organisation's culture were that had a negative effect, 55 per cent of teachers stated they did not feel appreciated and 51 per cent said they were not supported. These factors were above poor levels of workload (49 per cent) and work–life balance (45 per cent). In contrast, of those teachers who stated that their organisational culture positively impacted their wellbeing, good staff relationships, good leadership and feeling appreciated were given as key reasons for this. So while we may lay partial responsibility for poor teacher wellbeing on external factors, we must look to ourselves as school leaders to consider what we can do to better support and value colleagues. There are numerous aspects of school culture that leaders do have the ability to control and change to positively impact staff wellbeing that go beyond the tokenistic gestures. Supporting staff wellbeing involves being intentional and deliberate about the systems and structures we embed in our organisations in order to create a thriving school culture for all. For example, what are the systems and structures in place for teachers to collaborate and build relationships with each other? How might staff seek support to enhance their personal and professional skills without high-stakes accountability?

One way we might do this is by exploring teacher autonomy over professional development (PD). In an NFER report on teacher autonomy and job satisfaction and retention (2020, p. 18), Van den Brande and Worth found that 'teachers' perceived autonomy over their professional development (PD) goals has the greatest association with improved satisfaction and intention to stay in teaching'. When teachers are treated like the professionals they are and are able to engage and immerse themselves in effective continual professional development (CPD), then job satisfaction increases. It is therefore central that in order to improve teacher wellbeing, school leaders scrutinise their current CPD offers and contemplate on its effectiveness in building teacher autonomy.

STRATEGIES TO SUPPORT TEACHER WELLBEING

As a sector, we need to move away from tokenistic gestures which aim to 'support' teachers to manage their workload and promote positive wellbeing. I feel as though we are at a tipping point within the profession and the current state of teacher retention and recruitment means that school leaders must act now if we are to create sustainable schools for the future generation. It will take a collective and concerted effort; I think it is within the control of those who have the role and responsibility to do so such as governors, headteachers and school leaders, including middle and senior leaders.

However, nothing will change until leaders build a school culture where staff can be honest and transparent without the fear that they will be ignored, ostracised or mistreated. This benefits everyone, but particularly people with protected characteristics and minoritised groups.

In *The Fearless Organization* (2019, p. xvi) Amy Edmonson defined psychological safety 'as a climate in which people are comfortable expressing and being themselves. More specifically, when people have psychological safety at work, they feel comfortable sharing concerns and mistakes without fear of embarrassment or retribution.' As a leader, how do you provide space for all teachers to express their ideas, give feedback and share concerns about workload issues and their mental health and wellbeing? If you do so already, how do you respond to this in a manner that makes teachers feel listened to, valued and supported rather than maligned?

To begin, I propose providing multiple opportunities and modes for staff to share their opinions throughout the academic year.

GATHER STAFF VOICE

To retain teachers, we must establish clear systems and structures that enable staff to uphold positive behaviour in lessons and during unstructured times. Student behaviour and the admin linked to it significantly contribute to teachers' rising workload and poor mental health (DfE, 2024).

One suggestion is to identify unnecessary workload through anonymous staff surveys conducted weekly or termly, ensuring regular feedback rather than annual check-ins. This prevents staff from perceiving the process as performative and fosters trust in leadership's commitment to addressing concerns.

Surveys should allow staff to propose solutions, not just highlight problems. Online platforms like TeacherTapp and School Surveys can help tailor surveys to your school. Once collected, data must lead to action. Leaders should explore solutions through research and evidence-based strategies. A working party with a diverse range of colleagues can help co-design changes, ensuring staff feel heard and invested. While leaders may naturally engage those eager to contribute, it is equally important to include dissenting voices.

Many teachers share feedback with vulnerability, hoping for change, only to see no action or acknowledgement. As leaders, we may dismiss concerns raised by a few individuals, assume solutions are unmanageable, or fear disruption. However, failing to acknowledge concerns can be more damaging than ignorance. The summary report of the WLTL (DfE, 2024) found that teachers considering leaving cited feeling unheard by policy-makers as a contributing factor.

Ignoring staff concerns erodes trust and damages school culture, leading to teacher attrition. Stephen Covey's *The Speed of Trust* (2006) introduces four cores of credibility: integrity, intent, capabilities and results – essential for building and maintaining trust. Covey defines integrity beyond honesty, incorporating congruence, humility and courage. Leaders must communicate with integrity when addressing workload and wellbeing.

Consider the questions below to reflect on your approach to gathering and acting on staff voice.

- Have you gathered staff voice on workload and wellbeing concerns?
- How do you analyse and share staff voice data?
- How do you respond to feedback that challenges your perceptions?
- How often do you make changes based on staff voice?
- Are you transparent about both positive and negative feedback, or do you highlight only selected points?

Ensuring staff feel heard and valued strengthens school culture, enhances trust and improves retention. Leaders must be proactive in reducing workload burdens and fostering a supportive environment.

TACKLE BEHAVIOUR

As I shared earlier in this chapter, student behaviour and the admin linked to it significantly contribute to teachers' rising workload and poor mental health (DfE, 2024). To retain teachers, we must establish clear systems and structures that enable staff to uphold positive behaviour in lessons and during unstructured times.

The Education Endowment Foundation's guidance report *Improving Behaviour in Schools* (2021) offers brilliant recommendations. They emphasise building awareness of pupils and their influences through effective relationships. A relational approach to the behaviour policy is essential because sanctions alone do not create psychological safety or belonging for students and staff.

Overcomplicated behaviour policies make it difficult for teachers to apply expectations consistently. Some staff I spoke to shared that their school's behaviour policy had not been referenced since the first day of the academic year, making it hard to recall and follow. A policy must be consistently communicated to become applied practice.

If multiple staff members do not understand what to do in a specific incident, it is crucial to clarify the policy rather than blame them. One effective approach is allowing teachers to contribute to reviewing and adapting the policy. While a senior leader may oversee behaviour, involving staff empowers them and helps them align with policies. This addresses concerns that teachers feel their opinions are disregarded, which contributes to attrition.

Once a clear policy is established, communicate and review it throughout the year via staff briefings, student assemblies, or bulletins. Sharing it once is insufficient. A one-page document summarising key rules, routines, rewards, consequences, escalation procedures and parent communication can be helpful.

In my former role as an interim deputy headteacher, staff voice revealed that unclear punctuality policies led to persistent lateness without consequences. To address this, I created a visual one-page policy document, shared it in weekly briefings, assemblies and with families. This led to improved teacher buy-in and follow-through and reduced student lateness by end of the year. A similar strategy was effective in designing a mobile phone policy that significantly reduced behaviour incidents linked to mobile use.

Along with clear policies, staff must feel supported in enforcing them without fear of scrutiny. Some ECTs I interviewed worried that raising behaviour concerns would jeopardise their ECT year. They feared being blamed rather than supported. Psychological safety is critical – if teachers feel unsupported when reporting issues, they may avoid following policies altogether.

While multiple factors have contributed to deteriorating behaviour, leaders must consider how their daily interactions impact the school environment and staff wellbeing (Education Support, 2024). Reflecting on leadership practices can improve behaviour management. Asking colleagues for feedback can enhance self-awareness. The following questions might be helpful to reflect on.

- Do you role model the behaviour practice you wish to see from staff?
- Do you use interactions to promote the behaviour policy?
- How do you follow up on behaviour incidents?
- How do you support staff struggling with behaviour management without undermining them?

Many schools use On Call, where staff report behaviour during lessons which triggers support from senior or pastoral staff. However, some teachers report feeling undermined when students are removed but quickly returned without consequence, leading to further disruption. Social media teacher influencers even poke fun at some leaders – recounting stories of misbehaving students being returned to the lesson with rewards like lollipops. This leads to teachers feeling frustrated. The concern here is not the rewards themselves, but the perception that teachers' authority is being disregarded.

I am aware that some teachers require additional support to maintain high behaviour standards. Support frameworks work best in psychologically safe environments, and coaching and mentoring are key. More on this will be shared later in the chapter.

Beyond the classroom, corridor behaviour also increases teacher workload due to administrative tasks. As one teacher shared, 'sometimes it is easier to turn a blind eye to minor issues than to address misbehaviour on duty'. Reporting incidents was so time-consuming that they only intervened in cases of physical fights or verbal abuse. This reflects the burden of administrative red tape rather than the teacher's commitment to behaviour management.

A great example of simplifying behaviour administration comes from Forest Gate Community School, where I was previously an assistant headteacher. The school issued all staff a 'slip book' for corridor behaviour, with a duplicate copy system. One side listed merit-worthy behaviours; the other, demerit-worthy behaviours. Teachers recorded the student's name and form, handed one slip to the student, and submitted the duplicate to the admin team for input into behaviour software, which also notified families. This streamlined reporting while promoting a positive school environment.

Thus, I suggest working with teachers to explore how administrative tasks related to behaviour can be reduced, ensuring that staff feel encouraged to address and report misbehaviour efficiently.

TEACHER PROFESSIONALISM AND CPD

A key role that leaders play in schools is making decisions around teacher PD and ensuring its effectiveness in enhancing teacher practice. We know teacher PD can have an impact on student outcomes so the stakes can feel quite high, which can result in CPD being directed and presented by leaders instead of a more collaborative approach led by teachers themselves. However, research shows that 'teachers' autonomy over their PD goals is the most associated with higher job satisfaction' and that 'teacher autonomy is strongly related to the extent to which teachers regard their workload as manageable' (Van den Brande and Worth, 2020, p. 15). Despite this, teachers report that autonomy over PD is low. There may be a number of reasons for this which I will not be able to cover in this chapter. The key message though is that we must give teachers more control and choice over the CPD if we are to increase job satisfaction and hopefully enable staff to manage workload.

To support teachers in choosing their own PD goals, you might begin by amending your staff appraisal systems so that all targets are linked to teacher learning and research and away from performance-related pay. You might ensure that all teachers are assigned a coach outside the appraisal system to help them discuss and refine their PD goals without the fear of accountability that appraisal might bring.

In addition, teacher autonomy might also include providing teachers with opportunities to work towards their CPD goals by collaborating with the colleagues within and beyond their department or phase throughout the year. I have personally seen the impact of teacher collaboration on my own practice as a teacher and leader. As a third-year teacher, I worked at Little Ilford School in Newham where teacher autonomy linked to CPD was highly advocated. As part of this, teachers were given the choice to join one professional learning community (PLC), with each PLC focusing on a different teaching and learning priority such as assessment and feedback, literacy and numeracy and effective group work.

Once a term, staff would have the opportunity to meet in their PLC groups during directed time to share research, explore strategies and discuss impact to help enhance classroom practice. This was not just highly effective in improving my classroom practice, but also in building my expertise while encouraging me to connect with teachers beyond the English department. This did not mean that staff did not collaborate within their departments though. In fact, within the teaching timetable, all teachers were allocated joint planning time in addition to their usual planning, preparation and assessment (PPA) time. This involved having one lesson a week/fortnight allocated to all teachers to collaboratively plan lessons and schemes of work within curriculum areas. This was powerful in reducing my planning workload and improving my subject knowledge; it was also a highly enjoyable experience because I was able to build positive relationships with my colleagues (who are now my lifelong friends).

Good staff relationships is one way organisations contribute positively to staff mental health (Education Support, 2024). Surely, we therefore need to create further opportunities for staff to learn together. I believe that more opportunities like PLCs, joint planning time and coaching circles would go beyond the tokenistic wellbeing gestures of staff wellbeing events. This collaborative aspect of schools is reported to be declining with the OECD warning that 'this is dangerous, arguing that if schools are not "intellectually stimulating" places to work then "disillusionment may creep in ... teaching becomes far too unattractive to be counted among society's most respected professions"' (Bousted, 2022, p. 76).

Importantly, we must evaluate the impact of our current CPD offers and how far they create opportunities for collaboration and deep learning.

COACHING AND MENTORING

A key way of supporting staff to manage their workload and promote positive teacher wellbeing is by creating a culture of effective coaching and mentoring. As a school leader, I believe you have the power, agency and responsibility to support every member of staff to thrive in school. You can do this through regular line management or one-to-one meetings. We tend to think that line management only applies if you have a teaching and learning responsibility or a middle/senior leadership position. I think this needs to be an entitlement for all staff within a school setting as line management gives staff the space to express their ideas and be listened to, advocate for themselves and share updates and receive informal mentoring and coaching.

I know that teacher timetables, cover lessons and other issues make this a real challenge for school leaders; you might mitigate this by allocating line management time in lesson timetables when planning for the next academic year.

Effective line management includes: being clear in advance about key discussion points and actions; providing opportunities for teachers to share their thoughts and feedback; having coaching conversations to support them to explore different options open to them and giving teachers choice over those options. The role of line managers is also to mentor others. This means giving clear feedback that helps move people forward without apportioning blame. Kim Scott's *Radical Candor* (2017) is a fantastic book that explores how leaders might do this kindly and effectively.

Sometimes, colleagues will require more directive instruction based on your expertise. In order to encourage teacher autonomy, ask the colleague if they would like to explore options or would like advice. This will hopefully help them feel empowered rather than disillusioned. Beyond line management, schools should create a whole-school coaching culture to support workload and promote staff wellbeing. Coaching is built upon psychological safety and confidentiality.

To start, it is important to define coaching as there are many different types of coaching, particularly within the education sector. I use the definition offered by Campbell and Van Nieuwerberg:

A one-to-one conversation that focuses on the enhancement of learning through increasing self-awareness and a sense of personal responsibility, where the coach facilitates the self-directed learning of the coachee, through questioning, active listening, appropriate challenge and, when needed, practical guidance in a supportive and encouraging environment that leaves the coachee feeling clearer and more optimistic about the future.

(2017, p. 18)

I refer to this as executive coaching. This type of coaching provides a confidential space where the conversation is non-directive (unless necessary for the coachee) with probing questions asked by the coach to help the coachee seek solutions for themselves and achieve their goal. There is certainly a place for instructional coaching to help teachers develop their pedagogy and practice, but I believe that executive coaching programmes would be beneficial alongside instructional coaching and mentoring programmes.

Having established executive coaching programmes across a number of schools, I have seen first-hand the impact it has had in encouraging staff to not only manage their workload, but also enable them to think differently about themselves and others. For some colleagues, it has improved their self-awareness linked to their workload concerns; others have found it a useful space to discuss and solve problems. Coaches have mentioned how effective it was in helping them reflect and improve in and out of the classroom. For many participants partaking in the programme, they wished they could have more time with their coaches because they realised how powerful it had been for them (Bibi, 2021).

A core part of establishing a successful coaching programme is having highly skilled coaches. I was initially trained by an external coach, the brilliant Mary Philips at Sarah Bonnell School. There are now Level 5 Apprenticeships in Coaching like the one I am completing with the CVP Group and Diverse Educators that you or your staff could complete. By having in-house coaches, you develop your own staff and build capacity for others to eventually be trained by them, reducing the need for an external coach. Once you have trained staff, you need to decide who will be part of the pilot group. As the Lead Coach, I worked alongside the SLT team to discuss the priority groups for the pilot coaching and considered vulnerable and under-represented groups who might have required additional support or be over-represented in retention and recruitment data. For us, this included parents returning from maternity leave, people who were new to the organisation and those who were returning from long-term sickness. You might wish to select a different group based on your own retention and recruitment data. By providing colleagues who fall under these categories with a free coach, you demonstrate you value them by giving them a safe space to grow.

CONCLUSION

It is crucial for us to scrutinise what is happening within the walls of our state sector schools which is driving teachers out. As school leaders, we are at the forefront of not only addressing these problems, but also in creating and implementing the solutions. I have argued that we can support teachers to manage their workload and promote positive mental health and wellbeing by valuing staff voice, actively addressing disruptive student behaviour, promoting teacher autonomy through professional collaboration and providing effective lounge management.

We have more agency than we realise in implementing these changes and I hope that this will contribute a little towards improving the working conditions for teachers nationally and support teacher retention.

FURTHER LEARNING

- Campbell J. and van Nieuwerburgh C. (2017) *The Leader's Guide to Coaching in Schools: Creating Conditions for Effective Learning.* Thousand Oaks, CA: Corwin.

  I would highly recommend this book if you are seeking to improve the coaching culture within your organisation to improve the workload and wellbeing conditions for staff.

- Bibi Y. (2024) *A Little Guide for Teachers: Thriving in Your First Years of Teaching.* London: Corwin.

  My book offers insights into supporting novice teachers by providing strategies for effective classroom management, building professional relationships and maintaining a healthy work–life balance.

REFERENCES

Ainley, J. and Carstens, R. (2018) Teaching and Learning International Survey (TALIS) 2018 Conceptual Framework. *OECD Education Working Papers*, No. 187. Paris: OECD. https://doi.org/10.1787/799337c2-en

Bibi, Y. (2021) *The Power of Coaching: How to Embed a Whole-school Approach to Coaching*. Yamina Bibi Blog. Available at: www.yaminabibi.co.uk/post/the-power-of-coaching-how-to-embed-a-whole-school-approach-to-coaching (accessed: 20 March 2025).

Bibi, Y. (2024) *A Little Guide for Teachers: Thriving in Your First Years of Teaching*. London: Corwin.

Bousted, M. (2022) *Support Not Surveillance*. Suffolk: John Catt.

Campbell, J. and van Nieuwerburgh, C. (2017) *The Leader's Guide to Coaching in Schools: Creating Conditions for Effective Learning*. Thousand Oaks, CA: Corwin.

Covey, S.M.R. (2006) *The Speed of Trust: The One Thing that Changes Everything*. New York: Free Press.

Department for Education (DfE) (2024) *Working Lives of Teachers and Leaders: Wave 3 Summary Report*. Available at: www.gov.uk/government/publications/working-lives-of-teachers-and-leaders-wave-2/working-lives-of-teachers-and-leaders-wave-2-summary-report (accessed: 13 March 2025).

Education Support (2024) *Teacher Wellbeing Index*. Available at: www.educationsupport.org.uk/media/ftwl04cs/twix-2024.pdf (accessed: 6 May 2024).

Edmondson, A.C. (2019) *The Fearless Organization: Creating Psychological Safety in the Workplace for Learning, Innovation, and Growth*. Hoboken, NJ: Wiley. Kindle edition.

Education Endowment Foundation (EEF) (2021) *Improving Behaviour in Schools*. Available at: https://educationendowmentfoundation.org.uk/education-evidence/guidance-reports/behaviour (accessed: 4 May 2025).

McLean, D. and Worth, J. (2025) *Teacher Labour Market in England Annual Report 2025*. National Foundation for Educational Research. Available at: www.nfer.ac.uk/publications/teacher-labour-market-in-england-annual-report-2025/ (accessed: 14 March 2025).

Scott, K. (2017) *Radical Candor*. London: Macmillan.

Van den Brande, J. and Worth, J. (2020) *Teacher Autonomy: How Does it Relate to Job Satisfaction and Retention?* Teacher Development Trust. Available at: https://tdtrust.org/autonomy20/ (accessed: 16 March 2025).

INDEX

Page numbers followed by 'f' represents figure.

academic barriers, for ME students, 59–60
accredited providers, 38, 42
activist professionalism, 16–17
adaptability, 99
ADHD teachers, 79
administrative tasks, 128, 135, 141
advertisements, 38, 79, 126
agency, 4, 15, 82, 110
annualised hours, 126
anti-racist training, 75–76
Asian teachers. *See* minority and ethnic (ME) teachers
Atkinson, Elizabeth, 16
authentic leadership, 99
autistic teachers, 79, 83
autonomy, 2–3, 13, 109–110
   balancing support and, 115, 117
   case study, 28–31
   and professional development, 137, 141–142
   types, 26–27

Baker, Kenneth, 12
Ball, Stephen, 14
Bibi, Yamina, 5, 134
Black Papers, 12
Black teachers. *See* minority and ethnic (ME) teachers
Bousted, Mary, 135
Browne, Angela, 4, 69
budgeting/funding, 116, 122
Butterfield-Tracey, Polly, 2, 35

Callaghan, Jim, 11
career progression
   early career teachers (ECTs), 105, 112
   LGBTQ+ people, 94, 98
   minority ethnic groups, 60, 72
   need for, 17
   support staff into teaching, 41

Chartered College of Teaching (CCT), 2, 19, 23, 28
classroom management, 3, 109
coaching/mentoring, 5–6, 113–114, 142–144
collaboration, 5, 25, 30, 42, 83, 100, 112, 142
collegial autonomy, 26–27
"coming out", 96
communication, 99, 124, 135
compressed hours, 126
confidentiality, 143
connectivity, 99
Continuing Professional Development (CPD). *See* professional development
contrived collegiality, 30
Conyard, Gareth, 2, 9
Cook, Victoria, 2, 5, 23
corridor behaviour, 141
Courageous Leaders programme, 93, 100
Covey, Stephen, 139
Covid-19 pandemic, 135–136
credibility, 139
Crehan, Lucy, 17
cultural capital, 74–75
cultural influence, 59

data reporting, 135
Dawe, R., 30–31
DEIB. *See* diversity, equity, inclusion and belonging (DEIB)
discrimination, 4
   against LGBTQ+ teachers, 96
   minority and ethnic (ME) teachers, 72
disproportionality
   academic barriers for ME students, 59–60
   challenges, 56–58
   cultural and family influence, 59
   headteachers, 54–55f
   implicit bias, 60
   minority ethnic groups, 50–55
   negative school experiences, 59

by regions, 55–56
structural and systemic barriers, 60
student and teacher ethnic profile, 53f
teacher and pupil population, 52f
diversity, equity, inclusion and belonging (DEIB), 127–128
dyslexic teachers, 79

Early Career Framework (ECF), 3, 13, 107–108
Early Career Teachers (ECTs), 3, 36
　career progression, 105, 112
　experience, 108–109
　promises and realities of ECF, 107–108
　retention and progression, 109–113
　retention rate, 106–107
　strategies for school leaders, 113–117
　student behaviour, 136, 139–141
ECF. See Early Career Framework (ECF)
ECTs. See Early Career Teachers (ECTs)
Edmonson, Amy, 138
Education Endowment Foundation (EEF), 108, 139
Education in Schools Green Paper, 12
edu-influencers, 136
EEF. See Education Endowment Foundation (EEF)
effective teacher, 17
Ellis, Nansi, 2, 9
enquiring teacher, 17
Equality Act 2010, 93, 97
ethical leadership, 19
evidence-base practices, 15–16, 26, 109
executive coaching, 143

failures, learning from. See professional development
family influence, 59
The Fearless Organization, 138
fidelity, 15
Flex Education: A Guide for Flexible Working in Schools (book), 128
flexible working, 5, 39, 40, 122–123, 130
　DEIB, 127–128
　need for, 128–130
　recruitment, 125–127
　retention and wellbeing, 123–125
Forest Gate Community School, 141
Frostenson, M., 26

Gear, R., 29
gender identity, 93, 96
Gorard, Stephen, 3, 49
Gove, Michael, 14
government, and education, 10–11
great supply crisis, 106
GROW model, 86–87

Hargreaves, A., 30–31
Holloway, J., 30
homosexuality, 92, 95
human-centred leadership, 74–75

identity, 2, 3
implementation, 116–117
implicit bias, 4, 60
Improving Behaviour in Schools (EEF), 139
inclusive leadership, 69
　anti-racist training, 75–76
　cultural capital and human-centred leadership, 74–75
　institutional racism, 71–73
　intellectual racism, 73
　role models, 73
　senior leadership's colour-blindness, 72
　systemic barriers and teacher retention, 74
　teacher training and acceptance, 70–71
　under-representation in teaching workforce, 70
inclusive practices, 3–5, 60, 83–84
individual autonomy, 26, 27
inequalities, 4
Initial Teacher Training (ITT), 2, 35
　acceptance rate, 70–71
　ITT Market Review, 36, 38
　minority ethnic teachers, 56–57
INSET days, 12–13, 18
institutional racism, 71–73
instructional coaching, 143
insufficient support, 3, 107
integrity, 139
intellectual racism, 4, 72, 73
intensive training and practice (ITAP) elements, 36, 38
intersectionality, 83–84
intuition, 99
ITAP elements. See intensive training and practice (ITAP) elements
ITT. See Initial Teacher Training (ITT)

Japan, 18
job satisfaction, 1, 3, 5, 40, 107, 137
journal clubs, 6, 24, 27, 28–31

Keeping in Touch (KIT) days, 125

language, 81–82
leadership, 1
LEARNING Framework, 4, 80, 81f
　agency, 82
　approaches and challenges, 85–87
　environment, 82
　goals and benefits, 85
　inclusion and intersectionality, 83–84
　language, 81–82

nature, 83
neurodiversity-informed, 84
relationships, 83
Lee, Catherine, 4, 91, 98
lesson planning, 135
LGBTQ+ teachers, 4, 91
 conservative parents and governors against, 96–97
 educational setting, 94–95
 Equality Act 2010, 93, 97
 historical challenges, 92–93
 phase-specific inclusion, 97–98
 promoting curriculum, 95
 recruitment barriers, 93–94
 retaining, 98
 role models, 95–96
 as school leaders, 99–100
 Section 28 (1988–2003), 92–93
line management, 143
London, 70
London Borough of Lambeth's anti-racist framework, 75

Maxwell, B., 28
McGrath, J., 25
McNair Report, 10
mental health
 LGBTQ+ teachers, 98
 student, 135–136
 teachers' wellbeing and, 25, 98, 138–139, 142
Mezza, A., 25
microaggressions, 71, 74
mid-career teacher, 27
migration, 49
minority and ethnic (ME) teachers, 3–4, 49–50
 challenges, 56–58
 deputy headteachers, 54–55f
 discrimination, 72
 disproportionality, 50–55
 explaining under-representation, 59–60
 hidden workload, 74
 by regions, 55–56
 student and teacher ethnic profile, 53f
 teacher and pupil population, 52f
The Missing Mothers Report, 124
Moffat, Andrew, 4, 96–97
The Mother of All Pay Gaps online event, 127
MTPT Project, 125
Müller, Lisa-Maria, 2, 5, 23
multi-academy trusts (MATs), 20, 38–39

National Education Union's Anti-Racist Charter, 75
National Professional Qualification for Leading Teacher Development (NPQLTD), 44
National Professional Qualifications (NPQs), 13
nature, 83

negative experiences, 59, 71
neurodivergent teachers, 4, 78
 developing inclusive work environment, 80
 GROW model, 86–87
 recruiting, 79–80
 See also LEARNING framework
 supporting, 80
new professionalism, 25
No Outsiders programme, 95, 96–97
Now Teach, 127

Ofsted, 13, 40, 137
O'Neill, Claire, 4, 78
organisational culture, 72, 74, 76, 137
organisation types, 42
outdoor school spaces, 83
Ovenden-Hope, Tanya, 3, 105

Parcerisa, L., 30
parental cooperation, 135
part-time work, 39, 126, 129
Patience, Lindsay, 5, 122
pay gaps, 107, 116, 127
peer learning, 28
personal, social, health and economic (PSHE) education, 95
Philips, Mary, 144
policy-making, 2
practice-informed theory, 25
Pride and Progress, 93
primary education, 97
The problem of coming out, 96
professional development, 5–6, 27–28, 111–112, 137
 education policy and, 9
 enacting policy, 14–15
 future, 18–19
 journal clubs case study, 28–31
 for progression, 17–18
 and teacher identity, 15–16
 teaching as profession, 10–14
 time and space for, 114
professionalism
 conceptual framework, 24–25, 24f
 and CPD, 141–142
 definition, 18
 future of, 19
 progression, 17–18
 psychological safety, 138, 140, 143

Qualified Teacher Status (QTS), 38, 58
quality mentoring, 116

racial inequality, 4
racism, 71–73
Radical Candor (book), 143

Rasmussen, Mary Lou, 96
reality shock, 3, 108
recruitment, and retention, 1, 35–36
   budgeting/funding, 116–117, 122
   challenges, 106–107
   collaborative approach, 41–42, 45
   evolving ITT landscape, 38–40
   financial constraints, 116–117
   flexible working, 123–127
   inclusive practices, 3–5
   LGBTQ+ teachers, 98
   policy, and teacher professionalism, 2–3
   professional development and coaching, 5–6
   professional identity and autonomy, 23–28
   scenarios, 42–44
   school culture, 40–41
   school leaders strategies, 41, 44–45
   systemic barriers, 60, 74
   teacher shortage, 37–38
   workload, wellbeing, 5–6
reflective practices, 110–111, 114
reflective teacher, 17
relationships, 83, 142
remote working, 126
research and evidence, 115–116
RETAIN programme, 112, 115–116
role models
   LGBTQ+ teachers, 4, 92, 95–96, 100
   minority ethnic, 4, 55, 73–74
Rolfe's reflective framework, 86
Rose, Lucy, 5, 122
Ruskin Speech, 11

Sachs, J., 15, 25
Sackville-West, Vita, 95
Sadiq, Sufian, 4, 69
school-based initial teacher training providers (SCITTs), 38
school culture, 2–3, 138
   cultural capital, 74
   encouraging openness, 19
   growth-oriented, 112–113
   recruitment and retention, 40–41
   school leaders strategies, 114–115
school environment, 82
school leadership, 113–117
   balancing support and autonomy, 115
   diversity in, 60
   ECT development system, 113–114
   enhancing recruitment and retention, 41, 44–45
   growth-oriented school culture, 114–115
   implementation, 116–117
   LGBTQ+ teachers, 99–100
   recommended strategies, 44–45
   research and evidence, 115–116

School Surveys, 138
school teachers' pay and conditions (STPCD), 128, 131
SCITTs. *See* school-based initial teacher training providers (SCITTs)
Scott, Kim, 143
Scutt, C., 1, 26
secondary schools, 97
Section 28 (1988–2003), 92–93
See, Beng Huat, 3, 49
self-efficacy, 3, 107, 109–110, 114
sexual orientation, 93, 96
Shakespeare, William, 95
Sheppard, Emma, 124
Singapore, career progression in, 17
staggered hours, 126
Stonewall, 93
STPCD. *See* school teachers' pay and conditions (STPCD)
structural barriers, 60
structured autonomy, 115
student behaviour, tackling, 136, 139–141
Suarez, V. 25
subject hubs, 42, 44
supportive leadership, 4
Support Not Surveillance (book), 135
support systems, 74, 115
systemic barriers, 60, 74
Szamuely, T., 13

talent partnerships, 126
TALIS. *See* Teaching and Learning International Survey (TALIS)
teacher attrition, 37–38, 45, 106–107
teacher identity, 11, 15–16, 25
teacher professionalism, 2, 5, 24–27
   CCT model, 23–24
   raising profession through CPD, 27–28
   reimagining of, 15
TeacherTapp, 138
teacher training, 10, 12, 70–71
teaching
   future of, 18–19
   historical development of, 2
   as profession, 10–14
Teaching and Learning International Survey (TALIS), 51, 135
teaching and learning responsibility (TLR), 128
Teaching Quality White Paper, 12
teaching school hubs, 42, 44
time off in lieu, 126
traditional teaching, 12
transformative teacher, 17
truism, 18
Turing, Alan, 95

under-representation, of teachers
  minority ethnic, 50, 60, 69–70
  See also disproportionality
University and Colleges Admissions Service (UCAS), 56

wellbeing, 2, 5–6, 25, 137, 138
  coaching and mentoring, 142–144
  flexible working, 123–125
  LGBTQ+ teachers, 98
  staff voice, 138–139
  tackling student behaviour, 139–141
  teacher professionalism and CPD, 141–142
White spaces, 72
Wilde, Oscar, 95
Williams, Shirley, 12

Woolf, Virginia, 95
Working Lives of Teachers and Leaders (WLTL) survey, 40, 127, 135
work–life balance, 40, 107, 137
workload, 5–6, 126
  ECT stress, 108, 111
  expectations and teacher wellbeing, 2, 36, 138
  hidden, 74
  manageable, 113, 141–142
  reduction, 39–40
  stress, 134–136

Yang, Fujia, 3, 49

Zak, Paul J., 124